SMILE BANDAGES
Repairers of the Breach

SMILE BANDAGES
Repairers of the Breach

VERTIE PRINGLE-REID

Smile Bandages, Repairers of the Breach
Copyright © 2019 by Vertie Pringle-Reid. All rights reserved.

No part of this publication may be reproduced, stored in a retrieval system or transmitted in any way by any means, electronic, mechanical, photocopy, recording or otherwise without the prior permission of the author except as provided by USA copyright law.

The opinions expressed by the author are not necessarily those of URLink Print and Media.

1603 Capitol Ave., Suite 310 Cheyenne, Wyoming USA 82001
1-888-980-6523 | admin@urlinkpublishing.com

URLink Print and Media is committed to excellence in the publishing industry.

Book design copyright © 2018 by URLink Print and Media. All rights reserved.

Published in the United States of America
ISBN 978-1-64367-327-1 (Paperback)
ISBN 978-1-64367-326-4 (Digital)

General/Family/Church
28.03.19

DEDICATION

First and foremost, I dedicate this book and offer thanksgiving to my Lord and Savior Jesus Christ, whose blood was shed on Calvary; for that I also give the highest praise of Hallelujah.

My deepest gratitude, I offer to my mother, the late Sarah Virginia Pringle (1927-1976), who helped me to understand by the Scriptures that one should honor their parents.

I extend my love and appreciation to:

Those who honor me by calling me their "Mother"; whether they are my children by birth or those who are not my natural children.

My grandchildren, and to all of the children who call me "Grandma", and to those who know me as "Auntie".

Those who understand that by honoring their parents, that they are indeed honoring God.

Special dedication of this book is also extended to those of the upcoming generations who will be our heroes in the future.

CONTENTS

Preface...xiii
Author's Note.. xv
Chapter 1: Oh My God, What Have I Gotten Myself Into?.........1
Chapter 2: My Father's Business...7
Chapter 3: No More Stinky Diapers 21
Chapter 4: It's a God Thing 34
Chapter 5: I Learned the Hard Way..46
Chapter 6: Can You Hear Me Now?..55
Chapter 7: O Wretched Woman That I Am 69
Chapter 8: Hold My Bible 81
Chapter 9: Grandma's Vision: A Camp Ministry......................91
Chapter 10: Photo Gallery...102

YOU TAUGHT ME

You taught me, Lord, who I am and who I'm supposed to be
You showed me through the ones who
were to reveal Your love to me
A love I never knew existed before I learned of You
You taught me, Lord, who I am and what You expect of me

You taught me, Lord, to give to others,
especially those called by You
You opened doors and windows for Your blessings to come through
A God who cared enough to give His life for a wretch like me
You taught me, Lord, who I am and all that I could be

You taught me, Lord, that I'm blessed to give;
it doesn't matter when I don't receive
You lead me in the path that I should follow, to help those in need
A charge I have, while there's still time to
complete the task You've given
You taught me, Lord, to do for others and enjoy the life I'm livin'

You taught me, Lord, to be thankful for
everything You've done for me
You broke my bonds of sin and now I've been set free
A wonderful relationship has now developed between us two
You taught me, Lord, the steps to take, so that I can follow You

You taught me, Lord, the joy one has when living a life for You
You demonstrate Your love and strength, by the many things You do
A God who gave His only Son to shed His blood on Calv'ry
You taught me, Lord, if I abide in Your Word I can live for eternity

Vertie Pringle-Reid

WHAT MAKES A MOM A MOM?

Is it because she bore you? Birthed you? Nursed you? Carried you in her womb?"

It is the love that she gives, the way she lives before us...The care in her eyes and the tenderness in her voice.

It is the unselfish love and the need to love...her pure heart when she rebukes and the purity in her embrace.... Not just what she gives but how she gives it...All was bad...All was lost...All seemed over...Then her loving voice spoke tenderly to me...All will be well...Yes, that's a mom...

I came not from her womb but there is a cord that attaches us together that's stronger than the one cut at birth...It is the undying, everlasting, enduring, unfailing, unquenchable, cord of love...Momma Reid...poem exclusively and originally for you...

Written by Deatha Kirkland

Mother was the glue to the faithful few that kept us together while we were going through.

Confusion was in the atmosphere. Tomorrow we could not see... but through that lovely smile, we knew that God had a job for His child.

Prayers were going forth, dinners were being served, seniors, were blessed while Mother was being put to the test.

But oh how we were blessed through your faithfulness. We watched as you hemmed curtains, vacuumed floors, and we were always so happy to see you walk through that door.

Irreplaceable, phenomenal, virtuous, yes you are... In our eyes, Mother, you will always be a star... Proverbs 31:10...

Who can find a virtuous woman? For her price is far above rubies...

Written by Lisa Moore

PREFACE

While it is my purpose to expose the devil, his demons and their nasty workings that destroy people's lives, in my writings, I also want to inspire everyone to accept God's only begotten Son, Christ Jesus, who is the gracious gift that God offers to all of mankind. Most of the characters in my books have been taken from the Bible. I have then compared what took place in their lives with what is taking place in the lives of people today. The characters in the Bible have been deceased more years than I've been alive, yet, our mannerisms, deeds, and the situations in which we find ourselves are very much alike. Some of the non-biblical characters that I have written about are either deceased or are still living now during my lifetime. Plainly and honestly stated, the stories in my writings have not been written to offend anyone. My intention is to expose the workings of Satan and show that his attacks are aimed at killing or destroying the lives of others. I am also a target, as many of you are. We're all marked for destruction on the devil's hit list!

While holding onto my self-respect, I spent years trying to conceal the shameful things that had happened in my life and in the lives of some of my family members; things that I didn't want anybody to find out about, if they didn't already know. I was bound to secrecy because of my guilt. Satan had me in his clutches and I didn't even know it. I forced a smile to hide the suffering and shame that I did not want to be publicly exposed. I was stressed to the point of despair, almost losing my mind. When God came to my rescue, He completely healed and freed me to expose the strongholds by which the devil had me secretly bound. God gave me the strength to write about the things that I had been trying to keep private.

As you read about the vicious attacks of the devil, with prayer, you can be fortified by God's Holy Spirit to make a firm stand against the devil; the very enemy of our souls. I know that there are many people who are yet held bound by Satan, trying to cover-up the many unpleasant things that have happened in their lives. The Word of God tells us that we are to 'confess our faults to one another and pray for one another that we may be healed'. Silence forces us to suffer alone, but once that seal of secrecy is broken while casting our burdens of guilt on the Lord, Satan's power over us is broken. The Lord is more than willing to break Satan's strongholds in our lives when we repent of our wrong doings and walk towards His standards of holiness. I am witnessing, by my writings, to the truth of the freedom that God brings through His Son. He promises that 'whom the Son sets free, is free indeed'. (John 8:36) I don't want to cause fear, emotional pain or embarrassment, but these stories are indeed factual and need to be told.

AUTHOR'S NOTE

Reflecting back on my life, it is now more than thirty-seven years since I've offered God my time to be used in His service. I didn't think that the little I could do would have an impact in the lives of others. However, while first mothering my own children, then children of others, and those who God brought into my life, I've come to understand that through compassion, their lives have been changed by what I was able to contribute. As I've yielded myself to the Holy Spirit of God, my attitudes and behaviors changed so that others were able to see the love of Jesus through my life. The sharing of my faith in Jesus Christ has been more than a duty to me; it's been profitable to those who've come to accept Christ as their personal Savior through having witnessed the wonderful change that God brought about in my life.

My family, church members, neighbors and friends have favorably witnessed the gifts of service that God has brought to fruition in my life. As the youth leader and coordinator of two nursing home dance ministries, I've had many opportunities opened for me and the children in my two dance troupes to touch the lives of others with the love of God. The non-fictional books that I've authored have captured treasured memories from my distant and not-so-distant past; sketches of some of the challenges and obstacles that I've faced. Though compiling my autobiography has been therapeutic and stimulating to me, I find that living joyfully in the unfolding of God's plan for my life is exciting and refreshing to me everyday. I pray that through the reading of my books, others will be inspired and propelled into action to become foster care parents, who are our contemporary 'Repairers of the Breach'.

"Compassion Inspires Action"

Jesus' years of ministering demonstrate a never-ending love that inspires men and women, in the past and even today, to act compassionately towards those who are suffering. As recorded in the Holy Scriptures, through the life, death and the resurrection of Jesus, people have been dramatically influenced throughout the whole world. The compassion that was shown to those who suffered during Jesus' earthly life brings awareness to us that we also should have compassion on others by helping those who are suffering.

Evidence of Mother Teresa's love for God led her to help relieve the suffering that she saw in underprivileged people. She is known throughout the world for the compassion she showed to the poorest people during her lifetime. In one of Mother Teresa's recorded testimonies concerning her faith and love, she said . . .

"As to my calling, I belong to the world. As to my heart, I belong entirely to the Heart of Jesus. God still loves the world and He sends you and me to be His love and His compassion to the poor."

A woman known as Mother Hale began fostering other children during the time she was a young widow bringing up her own three children. She spent 52 years bringing hope and assistance to those who were less fortunate. Her life's greatest endeavor was the founding of Hale House; a home for drug-addicted and AIDS-infected children. The compassion that Mother Hale showed to those who suffered, gave hope to children while she lived and is yet giving hope to children today.

In one of Bishop Desmond Tutu's statements, he said, "*. . . in many ways, each one of us, of course, is expected to be an icon, an image of that which is invisible, an image of God, each one of us because we each have been created in the image of God. So people actually, if they want to know, "What is God like?" they would have to look at you and me and see us as being compassionate, because God is compassionate, as being loving, because God is loving. God is invisible. People wouldn't know about God except through those who are God's representatives, you and I and all of us.*" Reading biblical history about Jesus and the history about Mother Teresa, Mother Hale and Bishop Desmond Tutu in articles from Wikipedia Encyclopedia and the Academy of Achievement helped me to realize that all that we do is no less than what we've been called to do.

CHAPTER ONE

Oh My God, What Have I Gotten Myself Into?

In the late nineteen sixties, my mother and I were sure that I was in labor and ready to give birth. I was in a lot of pain in my back and lower abdomen, but I had already been turned away twice from the hospital. Without having done a thorough, physical examination on me, the doctor relied on questioning my mother and feeling my abdomen to try to determine if the baby had dropped into the birth canal. He told my mother that I was not in labor and that she should once again take me back home. Since this was my first pregnancy, I didn't have a clue as to what should be happening to my body if I were truly in labor. I was however crying because of the pain I was experiencing, and my mother told the Emergency Room doctor that she was not going to take me back home for the third time, until someone found out why I was in so much pain.

Another doctor came right away and I was examined thoroughly. This doctor realized that the baby was in a breech position, and immediately insisted that the nurses begin preparing me to be taken upstairs onto the Delivery Room floor. My street clothes were exchanged for a crisp, clean hospital gown, and I sat on the stretcher with my legs hanging off the sides. I tucked my legs up on the stretcher as the side rails were pulled up for my safety. As soon as I lay back unto the stretcher, two big, black, burly orderlies began pushing the stretcher as fast as they could towards the elevator doors.

Then up to the Delivery Room floor we went. Mom had followed quickly behind the stretcher right into the Delivery Room. I saw about six different doctors dressed in their starchy, white uniforms huddled around in the Delivery Room. There were probably nurses in there also, but I couldn't distinguish them from the doctors with the glaring lights in my eyes. I heard doctors discuss about the baby needing to be turned around from its breech position in order to be born without damaging me.

I was filled with extreme anxiety and fear. I grabbed hold onto one of the side rails of the stretcher and began shaking it violently while jumping up and down like a monkey. My tears were burning my eyes and streaming hot down my cheeks. I was screaming at the top of my lungs and crying all at the same time. I frantically searched the room with my eyes, desperately looking for my mother, but I couldn't find her. They probably had rushed her out of the room, then turning their attention back towards me; they tried to calm me down. It was one of the most frightening things I'd ever experienced when the doctor approached me with a big, long needle and told me to turn around so that he could stick that needle into my spine. He warned me to be perfectly still and not flinch lest a misplacement of the needle should cause me to end up paralyzed.

I often think back to that late night, around 1 o'clock A.M., of March 6, 1968. Had not my mother insisted that the doctors find out what the problem was, it could have been fatal for my baby as well as for me. I experienced many complications almost losing my life. I'd gone through my entire pregnancy without prenatal care. There had to be a turning and repositioning of the baby so that both of us could survive the trauma of the birthing process. Since, my breech birth experience, I've heard that many women have experienced breech pregnancies, but through prenatal care they have suffered little or no complications. Before that night that almost became fatal for me and my child, breech births were meaningless to me. I've later learned about a different kind of breach, that's now, in some cases, becoming fatal for mothers and children throughout our states.

I became aware of this kind of breach when an eleven year old girl was brought to me by a Division of Youth and Family Services

(DYFS) worker. It was around 10:30 pm when she was brought to my home with all of the belongings that she owned in one large, black garbage bag. Just looking at the child I felt sorry for her, but I didn't know how to approach her, so I asked her if she wanted something to eat. She responded by shaking her head saying no, but I caught a glimpse of a smile on her face.

Afterwards, I took her upstairs and showed her where she would be sleeping. I showed her where the bathroom was, gave her a washcloth, bath towel and a new bar of soap. I left her alone to prepare herself for bed and I went back downstairs, flopped into my easy chair, put my hands up to my head and said to myself, "Oh my God, what have I gotten myself into? What am I going to do with this eleven year old, pitiful looking girl? She looked as if she doesn't have a friend in the world." I did find comfort in the fact that the caseworker said that this child's placement with me would be only temporary. I didn't know how I would deal with an eleven year old child who had been separated from her family from the time she was two or three years old. How could I prepare myself to stand in the gap for a young person whose relationship had been breached between herself and her natural mother from the time she was a toddler? Accepting this lonely adolescent girl into my home and into my heart signaled a new direction for my ministry of love to include being a "repairer of the breach."

When I was a young girl growing up, my mother used Scriptures from the Bible to chastise me and my siblings. The one that she used most often suggested that if she spared the rod with us, we'd become spoiled. My mother was a single mom, raising seven children, and she used whatever methods she could to make us behave better. She told us that the Bible says that if we honor our mother and father that we would live a long time. One of her favorite warnings to us when we misbehaved and didn't heed to her warnings was, "I brought you into this world and I'll take you out of this world!" I gave my mother the utmost respect. I'm positive that I obeyed my mother's wishes after an understanding between us had been established. I'm not sure which dilemma I feared more: my mother 'taking me out of the world' or that God would shorten my life.

> *Ephesians 6: 1-3 "Children, obey your parents in the Lord: for this is right. Honour thy father and mother; which is the first commandment with promise; That it may be well with thee, and thou mayest live long on the earth."*

I realized, even as a child, that by having an understanding and a good relationship with my mother, that my life could be spared; assuring me that I'd live to become an adult. I did what my mother asked me to do, and for the majority of times that was true. I thought that I was fairly good. My relatives had even given me the reputation of having a 'heart as good as gold'. However, after I'd become an adult and read in the Bible that "...all of our righteousnesses are as filthy rags..." (Isaiah 64: 6), I realized that I didn't understand much about how God viewed things. I had not studied God's Word to know that I should let the mind of Jesus Christ be in me, and to have it soak into my mind. It was only after reading the passage in the Holy Bible that says, *"Thy word have I hid in mine heart, that I might not sin against thee"* (Psalm 119:11), that I saw the necessity of depending on God's Word for right living. Previously, when I had found myself in difficult situations, not knowing for sure what was right or wrong, I relied on my own senses of what I thought was the right thing to say or do.

My first acknowledgment of someone whose power was even greater than my mother's took place when I had an encounter with God during an out of body experience, while I was giving birth to my first child. The baby was turned crosswise in a position causing me to have what is known as a 'breech birth'. I thought I was about to die during that painful birthing episode. While I was in the hospital giving birth to my baby, death was hovering over me. That's when I knew for certain that God was not just a figment of my imagination. Laying flat on my back, helpless, unable to move, I knew that God is real. I realized that God has the power of life and death, and I knew that both my baby and I could have departed from this life. Now, whenever I hear someone talking about having an encounter with

God in a near death experience, my mind goes back to that night of March 6, 1968.

Hearing someone's description about a 'tunnel and indescribably bright lights,' I'm reminded of similar occurrences that I had experienced. Had I not read the account in the Bible, (2 Corinthians 12:2), where the apostle Paul describes a man that he knew, 'whether in the body or out-of-body', as being caught up to the third heaven, it would be hard for me to believe that an 'out-of-body', experience had really happened to someone. I probably would have thought that the person was describing a dream. However, by reading about it in the Word of God and by my own experiences, I actually do believe that someone's account of an 'out-of-body' experience is more than just a dream or imagination.

There was a time that I had doubts about the accuracy of certain events mentioned in the Holy Bible. I was somewhat like the disciple who could not believe the accounts that were told to him that Jesus was alive again from the dead unless he saw with his own eyes the nail prints in Jesus' hands and feet and actually touched the wound in His side. That disciple is known by many as 'doubting Thomas'. After that disciple was assured by his own senses; being able to see and touch the wounds in Jesus' hands and side, he fully acknowledged Jesus as his Lord and his God.

> *John 20: 25,27,28 "...But he said unto them, Except I shall see in his hands the print of the nails, and put my finger into the print of the nails, and thrust my hand into his side, I will not believe. Then saith he to Thomas, Reach hither thy finger, and behold my hands; and reach hither thy hand, and thrust it into my side: and be not faithless, but believing.... Thomas answered and said unto him, My Lord and my God."*

Thereafter, Thomas went forth to preach the gospel, and the testimonies of his experiences are recorded for us in the Scriptures. My experiences with God convinced me that Jesus is really who the Holy Bible describes Him to be, and I also recognize Him as my Lord and my God. I am determined to share the gospel with the same conviction that the early disciples had.

> *John 20: 30, 31 "… many other signs truly did Jesus in the presence of his disciples, which are not written in this book: But these are written, that ye might believe that Jesus is the Christ, the Son of God . . ."*

CHAPTER TWO

My Father's Business

I often got into trouble for talking too much, when I was a young child. My mother, teachers, and many other well meaning people would say things like "mind your business" or "you are always doing something that you have no business doing". So, over the years of hearing those words I became shy and withdrawn. I didn't know how much was enough to say or how much was too much to say. Nor did I have a clear understanding of what business I should be doing. I read in the Holy Bible that Jesus was twelve years old when He was found in the temple speaking with the religious elders about things concerning His heavenly Father. I felt that I also should be minding my heavenly Father's business after I accepted Jesus as my personal Savior.

I began to share with others about God's plan of salvation for them. After my born again experience, I began focusing on the kind of lifestyle that would be pleasing to God and I began preaching God's Word by the way that I lived. It wasn't always easy, but as I learned God's Word, I began practicing God's Word in just about everything that I did. I've often imagined myself in someone else's situation and I've begun using the "what if" phrases, such as: "What if the problem or situation that another person was experiencing was happening to me or to someone who I cared about?" "What if I was in prison? What if I was hungry? What if I was sick? What if I didn't have the proper clothing to wear? How would I want someone to respond to me?" (*Matt 25: 35-46*)

Questioning myself and using "what-if-situations," often led me to make decisions that I thought would be honoring God. (*2Cor 13: 5*) I felt that God would know that I was truly Christ-like by the good things that I was doing for others. I constantly did something good for my family members, as well as for those who were not members of my immediate family. I especially helped those who were seeking to have a relationship with the Lord and were unable to do for themselves. I gave out of my own resources to meet their needs. The more I did for others, the more genuinely I began caring about them. As I received financial blessings, I was able to reach out to my extended family and friends. I treated them as if they were my very own children. I exercised the gift of motherly love and I cherished it. As my faith developed even more, I understood the compassion that led Jesus to help people according to their needs. With motherly love and compassion, I reached out to help those who came across my path.

> *Matt 14:14 "…Jesus went forth, and saw a great multitude, and was moved with compassion toward them, and he healed their sick."*

Subtle changes at different times in my life seem to have catapulted me eventually into the will and design that God purposed for me. In my early childhood, I made up my mind and was determined how I was going to live my life once I moved out from my mother's house. I couldn't wait until I became an adult so that I could do all the things that I wanted to do. So when I finally reached adulthood, I began doing many of those morally wrong things that I had seen other adults doing. Not wanting anyone to think that I wasn't a respectable person, I practiced those things privately.

After sometime, I began thinking that there should be more to my life than just looking forward to drinking and partying on the weekends. However, I enjoyed my life. I looked forward to hanging out on the weekends drinking and partying with my friends. As an adult, I never even considered that I would have to answer to anyone about what I did with my life. It was my business whatever kind of lifestyle that I lived. When I was a child, I had done what I thought was the right things to do, according to somebody else's view of right things.

I had believed that Santa Claus could see, hear, and that he knew everything about me. I had been told that if I was good I would be rewarded with gifts, so I had tried to be good so that he would bring me the presents that I had asked him for in my letters to him. When I first came to the point of believing in God's existence, as an adult, I tried to impress Him, just like I had tried to impress Santa Claus when I was a child. I began doing things that I thought were morally and ethically right just to cover up those areas that I knew were wrong.

Now that I was a Christian, I had to be careful about the lifestyle that I lived. I knew that my life was not my own any longer; I was bought with a high price, which cost the life of God's only begotten Son, Jesus Christ. There's a story in the Bible that tells about a king who planned an extravagant wedding feast for his son. The king sent his servants out to invite some guests who disqualified themselves with their lame excuses. When the servants reported their responses back to the king, he became furious, and commanded his servants to "*...go into the roads leading out of town and invite as many people as you can find to the wedding. Those servants went out into the streets and brought in all the people they found, evil and good alike, and the wedding hall was packed with guests*". (Matt 22: 9, 10)(International Standards Version) Although suitable wedding attire was available for all of the attendees, one man slipped in amongst the invitees still wearing his old dirty clothes. When the king noticed that improperly dressed man, he demanded to know "*...Friend, how camest thou in hither not having a wedding garment?*" That man must have known by the king's question that he was in deep trouble; he had no answer for the king "*...he was speechless.*" (Matt 22: 12) The king, in his fury, demanded his servants to "*...Bind him hand and foot, and take him away, and cast him into outer darkness; there shall be weeping and gnashing of teeth. For many are called, but few are chosen.*" (Matt 22:13, 14)

God is preparing a grand wedding feast for His Son and His Son's bride. Invitations to attend that gala event are being carried, even now, into the highways and byways of life to compel all to make ready to attend the greatest event that is yet to come, the marriage supper of God's Son. The wedding garments of holiness and righteousness have been bought and paid for with the precious, shed blood of the Son of God who died on Calvary's tree. Those garments are freely available to all who will accept the invitation to the marriage feast of Jesus Christ, the Lamb of God. His bride has already begun to adorn herself with the garments of holiness and righteousness; she is none other than that universal body of faithful believers, the church.

> *Isaiah 61:10 I will greatly rejoice in the LORD, my soul shall be joyful in my God; for he hath clothed me with the garments of salvation, he hath covered me with the robe of righteousness, as a bride groom decketh himself with ornaments, and as a bride adorneth herself with her jewels.*

The more that I read in the Bible, about the wealth, beauty, joy, peace, happiness, health and security of heaven, and reading that the causes for the tears of sorrow would be wiped out; even death itself being eradicated, I began to mature as a Christian. It's enough reward for me now, just to know the sure promise of having a place prepared for me in heaven. Yes, heaven's a wonderful place and I'm looking forward to getting there to see my Savior's face.

As the oldest of my mother's seven children, I had been helping with my siblings since I was eight years old. I watched out for my brothers and sisters as my 'Mama's little helper'. Whenever my mother prepared a whole chicken for our dinner, we'd only have enough to go around if the chicken's back was included as a portion. Knowing that the one chicken was all that we had, I told everyone that I liked the chicken's back best of all, so that everyone would have a piece of that chicken. Long after we could afford to have two chickens for dinner, I went without eating a choicer portion of the chicken; still eating the chicken's back. Either I had started believing that lie I'd told, or I had begun liking the chicken's back best of all. I don't know why I never straightened out that lie and told them that I would've liked to eat the leg, wing, breast or thigh, at least sometimes.

I shutter sometimes when I think about how many lies that Satan had deceived me with during my childhood. Those lies could have boomeranged, and caused me to have been lost for all eternity. As a child, I had received Christmas presents, supposing that they had come from Santa Claus. At Easter, I had received a basket full of colorful eggs and candies, supposing that they had come from a large pink and white bunny rabbit. Those skillfully devised demonic lies could have backfired, causing me to reject the truth about the death, burial, and resurrection of Jesus Christ. It's a miracle that I believed and received Jesus as my personal Savior after having been deceived about Santa Claus and the Easter Bunny.

However, when I read about Jesus and the devil and about heaven and hell, I believed what I read, and came to the decision that I had better do what I thought God would count as righteousness. The Bible says that hell is a horrible place, made for the devil and his demons, not for people. But, hell has enlarged itself to accommodate those who will not accept the Savior into their lives. I remember hearing grown-ups saying to someone who'd done something wicked, that they'll "burn in hell" for what they'd done. I was convinced of the reality of both heaven and hell by what I'd read, and by what I'd heard. That's what scared me straight. I remember seeing a documentary where a group of youths had been taken on the inside of a prison to see what life was like for the inmates who had committed horrible crimes. Many of the youths were so frightened after meeting those prisoners and hearing about their crimes, that the direction of their lives was forever changed. They were scared straight by the reality of what could happen to them if they continued on their present lawless paths. According to the Word of God, if I make the right choices in my life and have the right motives, I can rightfully expect to receive the promised rewards.

> *Galatians 6:9, 10 "Let us not lose heart in doing good, for in due time we will reap if we do not grow weary. So then, while we have opportunity, let us do good to all people . . ." (New American Standard Bible)*

My mother never told me that when I was born, that I was any different from any of her other children that she had given birth to. Therefore, I assumed that I was just an ordinary baby. I grew up doing childish things. I wasn't born with the mind to do the things that God designed me to do. It was only after I became a born-again Christian that I sought, through the reading of God's Word, to have the mind of Christ. Being born-again has changed how I feel about God's Word and about other people. Ordinarily,

I would only think about my own needs and the needs of my own family. After being born-again, I am also concerned about the physical and spiritual needs of others.

> *Philippians 2: 4, 5 "Don't be concerned only about your own interests, but also be concerned about the interests of others. Have the same attitude that Christ Jesus had". (God's Word Translation)*

Having my mind renewed by the Word of God, my entire life has been transformed. Now, not only do I think about having my physical needs met, but many times I help others get their physical needs met so that they can be more receptive when I talk to them about the gospel. I'm genuinely interested in helping others to come to the saving knowledge of Jesus Christ. I began caring for children and adults with disabilities as my way of extending help to those who aren't able to care for themselves. I know God sees me and He's giving me wonderful opportunities to extend myself to people less fortunate. I've even imagined that a few angels may have been disguised as people assigned to report back to God whether or not I've treated them with kindness.

SMILE BANDAGES, REPAIRERS OF THE BREACH

> *Hebrews 13:2 "Do not neglect to show hospitality to strangers, for by this some have entertained angels without knowing it". (New American Standard Bible)*

Everything that I have belongs to the Lord; my heart, mind, soul and my earthly possessions. When someone in need approached me, asking for my help, I willing gave it without giving it a second thought. Having the mind-set that all I possess belongs to the Lord; I've never felt that I was being used or taken advantage of. That way of thinking has made it easy for me to give assistance to anyone who asked for my help. My time, prayers, and even some godly advice are also freely given.

In some cultures, guests, upon entering another's home, are told "come-in and make yourselves feel at home". At one time I thought that was just polite hospitality, not to be taken literally. However, after becoming a born-again Christian, I literally welcomed into my house strangers and friends alike saying, "Make yourselves at home". When friends have brought along someone with them to visit me, I warmly welcomed them into my home.

> *Luke 6: 32-36 For if ye love them which love you, what thank have ye? for sinners also love those that love them. And if ye do good to them which do good to you, what thank have ye? for sinners also do even the same. And if ye lend to them of whom ye hope to receive, what thank have ye? for sinners also lend to sinners, to receive as much again. But love ye your enemies, and do good, and lend, hoping for nothing again; and your reward shall be great, and ye shall be the children of the Highest: for he is kind unto the unthankful and to the evil. Be ye therefore merciful, as your Father also is merciful.*

The Bible tells of a man who came to see Jesus under the cover of night; a Pharisee, a ruler of the Jews, whose name was Nicodemus.

He knew Jesus was from God because of the miracles Jesus had done. While having a conversation with Jesus, Nicodemus was told that a person had to be born-again in order to see the Kingdom of God.

> *John 3: 3-7 Jesus answered and said to him, "Truly, truly, I say to you, unless one is born again he cannot see the kingdom of God." Nicodemus said to Him, "How can a man be born when he is old? He cannot enter a second time into his mother's womb and be born, can he?" Jesus answered, "Truly, truly, I say to you, unless one is born of water and the Spirit he cannot enter into the kingdom of God. "That which is born of the flesh is flesh, and that which is born of the Spirit is spirit. "Do not be amazed that I said to you, 'You must be born again.'(New American Standard Bible)*

Nicodemus came and sought out Jesus believing that He was from God because of the miracles that Jesus had done, however, he questioned the born again experience. Through faith, I believed that God sent His only begotten Son so that I could be born of His Spirit and enter into God's kingdom. As a new born babe in Christ, I studied God's Word in order to be well-informed of the Scriptures. After a few years, my pastor ordained and licensed me to preach the gospel as an evangelist. During the early years of my maturing as a Christian, my first priority was raising my children. God's Word was the manual that I used and closely followed to train up my children.

I'd heard that God has a sense of humor, but I didn't give it any real thought until my life began unfolding. While raising my son and three daughters I said to myself, more times than I can remember, "Once they're adults, I'll answer the call of an evangelist". I thought evangelism would be much more stimulating than just staying at home rearing my children. The vision of working in the field of evangelism seemed to be so far off, yet I felt that I needed to postpone 'the call of evangelism' until my children were grown and out on their own.

In the meantime, whenever there was a need to chastise or correct any one of my children, I would lecture them from the Bible. Without my realizing it, I was really doing the work of an evangelist with my own children. After my children were adults, I became a foster parent, mothering other women's children. When I realized that I had four foster children, a little girl and three little boys at the same time, I joked with the Lord by saying, "Either I did a bad job raising my own children, and You considered it as a practice run, so now You want me to do it again to see if I'll get it right; or, I did such a good job raising my own children so that now You want me to do it again raising other people's children so that I can show others how to do it to honor You." During those precious years while raising my children, I spoke freely to the Lord; like two friends would speak to one another, for He had become my best Friend. However, I really had no intentions of raising more children.

Yes, I do indeed think that God has a sense of humor. God has me now sharing the same kind of motherly love to mentally challenged adults and to the children in my foster care that I had shown to my own children during the years that I faithfully followed God's instructions found in His Word, the Bible. As God's plan for my life slowly unfolded, I was smoothly and effortlessly transitioned into the full reality of the vision of evangelism that God had imparted to me so many years before while my children were yet very young.

> *John 15:11 "These things have I spoken unto you, that my joy might remain in you, and that your joy might be full. John 17:13 And now come I to thee; and these things I speak in the world, that they may have my joy fulfilled in themselves."*

With the sudden death of my mother, no one in our family was willing or even able to care for my brother Bob. He had experimented with drugs in his early teens, which caused him to have some serious mental problems. Bob's behavior brought to my mind a man mentioned in the Scriptures who was possessed with demons until

Jesus set the man free by casting those demons into a herd of swine that then ran over a cliff and drowned in the sea below.

Bob was my brother, and I was the oldest of my mother's children so the task of caring for him, after she died, became mine. Due to the demonic behavior and depression that held him captive, I was constantly challenged during the last twelve years of his life. Only God knew how terrified I was when the demons' activity flared up inside of Bob, changing his normally mild behavior into a tirade of agitation and aggression. I've come to realize that, had it not been for the years of experience that I gained while caring for my brother, I would not have been prepared to face and cope with the challenges presented by adults who struggle with psychological issues.

'Patience,' as well as 'change,' comes only with time; likewise, one cannot hurry the process for changes to take place in his or her life. I was a young mother caring for my own children and had no idea how I was going to take care of my mentally challenged brother in my home. I was angry with my mother for dying so young and I resented my brother because I had to take care of him. I felt like I didn't have a choice in the matter; it was expected of me to care for my brother. I thought that even though my mother was dead, she would have wanted me to take care of him. Like a spoiled child, I resented that chore that was forced upon me. I cried out in fits of anger to my deceased mother, "Why did you have to die and leave me to take care of your child?" I sulked and cried for hours, before I called out to God to help me cope with the new responsibility that had now fallen on me. I asked for God's forgiveness for my selfish and uncaring attitude towards my brother. I even asked to be forgiven for being so angry with my mother for dying. I pleaded with God to give me the kind of love that I needed to care for Bob.

As I began experiencing the healing power of God's forgiveness, He filled my heart with His pure, unconditional love that enabled me to minister un-hypocritically to my brother's needs. He also granted me understanding, guidance and wisdom. As God had granted ancient King Solomon with wisdom to make wise judgments concerning the people in his kingdom, God took away the resentment that had filled my heart and He replaced it with the love of Jesus to take care of my brother. Additionally, while caring for Bob, the 'patience of Job' was developed within me. My lifestyle changed drastically after I'd become a Christian; from the "fast lane" of bar-hopping with my former friends, to a much slower pace that allowed me to meet the special needs of the adults and children that were a part of God's plan for me.

> *Colossians 1: 21-23 "...you were alienated from God and were enemies in your minds because of your evil behavior. But now he has reconciled you by Christ's physical body through death to present you holy in his sight, without blemish and free from accusation-if you continue in your faith, established and firm, not moved from the hope held out in the gospel..." (New International Version)*

The Holy Spirit empowered me to sincerely show love to Bob. As I became aware of the increasing severity of his mental condition, I was able to judge wisely when dealing with his confrontational behaviors without taking offence. Many times my life was in jeopardy, but with the Holy Spirit having imparted wisdom to me, I was able to escape serious physical harm while keeping Bob from harming himself. Caring for Bob prepared me emotionally and physically to later be able to work with and care for other mentally disturbed adults. I now enjoy a lifestyle that lets me be patient with others and my charges can accompany me wherever I go. Along the way, while caring for Bob, I learned to be patient and to love unconditionally in spite of his unpredictable, erratic behavior. I developed sensitivity to his "hurts" that he was unable to put into words. Mentally challenged adults like my brother, suffer; being trapped and unable to escape their dementia.

I've learned many valuable lessons, down through the years, by listening to the voice of God and I've come to trust Him. As required by the law of the state, I had to take a couple of basic first-aid training courses before either medically fragile children or mentally challenged adults could be placed into my home. God's law, which is essential for me to care for these children and adults who need special care, is love. Respecting others, the same as I would want someone to respect me and also by loving my neighbors the same as I love myself, is God's 'love package'. Practicing God's standard of love, has prepared me to give not only proper supervision to my charges, but also to be a loving caregiver to them. Caring for my charges is not just a job; it's a labor of love. Stereotypes are often blamed for faulty views of foster parenting. While some children and adults may be abused physically or emotionally by some foster caregivers, the majority of these children and adults are given the love, care and attention that they need along with a sense of belonging that all human beings crave.

The handicapped children and adults who I care for are unable to verbally express their needs and desires. Working with them is very challenging. It was only after I'd raised my own four children and cared for my brother, that I felt a strong desire tugging at my heart to care for dependant children and adults. My heart's desire is to meet their needs and help them cope with and work through their problems and challenges. There were a few thoughts that merited my consideration that helped me to reach that decision for my life. First of all, I considered that God is the one who placed this sincere desire in my heart, and I'm now enjoying the rewards of being a loving caregiver and foster parent. Equally important, I considered that I might not always have the support and assistance that I might ask for from some of the agencies which sponsor the charges that I wished to care for. Thirdly, it was my determination and choice to make a positive difference in their lives, with God's help. Fourthly, also important, I considered that even in the most difficult and stressful situations I would have to depend and rely on God for His wisdom to help pull me through until the better times arrived.

In my day to day living, I respond to my own physical needs and desires with ease, and at the same time I must be alert and sensitive to respond to the needs of those who depend on me for their care. Those who are mentally challenged often don't have the skills necessary to interpret their own desires and urges and then communicate clearly to me. In various situations where a normal person would have no difficulty responding in culturally acceptable ways, these challenged individuals may respond inappropriately. As a dedicated caregiver, I am expected to observe my charges and follow-up on their body language in order to detect and meet their verbally unexpressed needs.

When I have an itch, I scratch it or I get someone else to scratch it if I can't reach the itch. When my neck or back muscles feel tense, I can ask for a neck rub or a back massage. When I want to be hugged, I can ask for it. I can even hug someone else appropriately, expressing my affection for them. My charges on the other hand have limited verbal communication skills. I remember when my brother Bob was just a little boy and I would often hug and kiss him affectionately, as an older sister would affectionately express her love for her younger brother and other siblings. As an adult, although he was mentally challenged, Bob still would come to me from time to time, for a hug and a kiss. Looking back on how I had cared for him, I realize that my charges today also need to be embraced with love and tender kisses, from time to time.

Although their verbal communication skills may be lacking, I encourage my charges to do for themselves; but with compassion, I do for them what they cannot do for themselves. According to their needs, I engage in bathing them, toileting them, dressing them, not only cooking for them but sometimes even putting the food into their mouths. On the lighter side we enjoy dancing to music, making funny faces and laughing together. Playing peek-a-boo is one of our favorite games.

During the summer months, we pick up food from a fast-food-drive-through restaurant and then we head out to Spring Lake Park to listen to the live free music concerts. On nice sunny days, we take leisurely strolls and we sit on the park benches to watch the people as they whiz by in their cars, trucks, or on their bikes. We watch the geese as they swim around in the pond, ducking their heads in and out of the water. Sometimes we get a chance to watch as traffic backs up as cars come to a screeching halt for a family of geese, in line formation, that are marching gingerly to the other side of the street.

One day when we were returning home from one of our outings, the sky quickly became overcast with dark puffy clouds that burst into unexpected showers. We locked our arms together as we ran from the van towards the house, laughing all the way. On the more serious side, I make sure that my charges get their yearly physical and dental screenings done. When emergencies arise, I get them the medical attention that they need and I make sure that all of their medications are taken as directed by their doctors. Although I assist my charges when necessary, I encourage them to strengthen and develop the capabilities that they do have. While I provide emotional support and physical assistance, as needed, they thrive in an environment that enhances their independence while I respect their rights to live up to their own potentials.

God, Himself, had demonstrated His supreme love by reaching out to mankind through His Son, Jesus Christ. God's love cost the precious life of His only begotten Son. Jesus said "*… whosoever shall lose his life for my sake and the gospel's, the same shall save it.*" (*Mark 8:35*) My immoral lifestyle was surely a path that could have led me to an early grave. Since accepting Jesus as my Lord and Savior, a change has taken place in my heart, and I'm now living on a path that experiences the blessings of God's promises for all those who practice righteous living. Not only by believing in God's unique Son do I have eternal life, but I'm blessed to be living a more abundant life now. (*John 10:10*) By yielding to the Holy Spirit, I give loving care to both children and adults in my charge; thus allowing them to experience God's abundant blessings. I'm being compensated even now as God provides me with good health, enabling me to care for them. Realizing that my ways please God, I'm at peace while I'm experiencing this unspeakable joy that comes from knowing that I have everlasting life.

> *John 3:16 "For this is how God loved the world: He gave his unique Son so that everyone who believes in him might not be lost but have eternal life." (International Standard Version)*

CHAPTER THREE

No More Stinky Diapers

God gives me much insight about love as I continue caring for mentally challenged adults and my foster children. I never thought that I'd have a greater understanding about how awesome His love is while I was in the process of changing a dirty diaper. One of my mentally challenged adults, who has Alzheimer's, needed to have his soiled diaper changed. The whole time while changing him, he was resisting me by his screams and by his efforts to push me away. After thoroughly cleaning him, he made another large BM a few moments later and I had to repeat the cleaning process all over again.

During this time, which seemed to take forever, I raised my voice "Be still! I should be the one crying, as stink as you are! Do you think I want to be changing your stinky diapers all the time?" I knew he didn't understand my sentiment, but God surely did. I heard the Holy Spirit quietly speaking to my irritated spirit. "How do you think sin smells?" All of a sudden I began to imagine that sin must stink in the nostrils of God too.

When we repent and are thoroughly cleansed by the blood of Jesus, and then begin to practice sin again, we need to be cleansed again. There's no difference in the stench from a smelly, dirty diaper and the stench that comes from sin in our lives. The young man, who has Alzheimer's disease, didn't realize that after his dirty diaper was changed, he would feel a whole lot better, but I sure did. It didn't matter how much he screamed for me to stop, he still had to be cleaned up in order to smell better and feel better. Likewise with us, we may not realize that by submitting ourselves to God and then resisting the devil that we will feel a whole lot better about being freed from the bondage of sin, but Jesus knows. We will experience a refreshing when we yield ourselves completely to the Holy Spirit.

Since my 'dirty-diaper-experience', I'm often reminded of God's love and faithfulness. Whenever one of my adults needs a cleansing, I am faithful to the task of removing the stench off of them; not only because I am their caregiver, but also because I love them. When we turn back and sin after we have been washed clean in Jesus' blood, our situation is described in *2 Peter 2: 22* as, "*… The dog is turned to his own vomit again; and the sow that was washed to her wallowing in the mire."*

I pictured a dog returning to the scene of his own vomit and eating it and a fat pig rolling in slop-drenched mud after someone had already washed her clean with a water hose. With those vivid recollections in my memory, I confessed and repented immediately, knowing that He is faithful to forgive me and cleanse me, all over again, from all of my unrighteousness. I know Jesus loves me.

> *1John 1:9, 10 "If we confess our sins, he is faithful and just to forgive us our sins, and to cleanse us from all unrighteousness. If we say that we have not sinned, we make him a liar, and his word is not in us."*

As the deer seeks after water to quench his thirst, I seek after my God to quench my thirsty soul. I sing songs of praise and adoration in my worship to the Lord. I love singing the song "I want to be like Jesus, I want to be like Jesus, so meek and lowly, so humble and holy, oh how I long to be like Him." Whenever I sing that particular song, I'm reduced to tears of rejoicing, having experienced the contentment that come from having such sweet fellowship with Jesus. My life has proven to be more satisfying and enriched by His presence, and that is more than I could have ever hoped for.

My relationship with the Lord grew in depth as I gradually answered His call to be mothering, first to my own children, then to children whom I fostered. It was years before I understood that God had prepared and equipped me for a task that would have been much too difficult had I not first been trained for it. Children and parents alike, experience the tragedy of loss and separation when their lives are thrown into unexpected turmoil and frustration. They are often forced, through circumstances, to be separated from one another. The culprit behind this mass confusion is Satan who enjoys stirring up chaos. He uses whatever he can to steal, kill and destroy human lives. Satan is on the rampage to destroy the whole human race. His mode of operation is to disrupt the family unit, which is the most basic building block of cultures and civilizations.

Many young children are orphaned or abandoned and left to fend for themselves on the streets, if they're not fortunate enough to be placed into government-subsidized foster care. Without proper instruction and guidance from a caring adult, or from a good role model, the children, more-than-likely, will themselves become unstable adults. Stability is necessary in young children's lives to prepare them to be able to cope with any obstacles or difficult situations that they might encounter as teenagers and later on as adults. The damage caused by children being separated from their biological parents can often be counteracted and minimized when a loving grandparent is available to care for their own grandchildren.

With many teenagers having children, their own parents may have difficulty transitioning into the role of grand-parenting. Many of these mothers are still mothering their other young children and are unprepared mentally, emotionally, physically and oftentimes financially to care for their child's offspring.

I am grateful to the Lord for having already raised my own children and seeing that they are responsible parents raising their own children. While enjoying my life of having grandchildren and spending some time as a grandmother with them, I was pleasantly surprised when I realized that I was being led by God to begin mothering more children. Years of preparation had taken place during those times that I considered to be the "best times of my life". I laughed often remembering the good times I had raising my children. Although I experienced a little sadness every now and then, the good times always out weighed the bad times. I even remember the laughter and joy that my children and I shared while I was caring for my brother, Bob. He was challenged mentally, yet, having him as a part of our family brought me immeasurable happiness. It had not been that way in the beginning, when he first came to live with us. However, nearing the end, before his death, God had completely transformed me. As I was being renewed in my mind and my heart, I began loving my brother unconditionally, the same as I loved my very own children.

A few years after my brother's death, I began caring for a young woman who was mentally challenged, who had some of the same behaviors that Bob had exhibited while I cared for him. Although she was much more paranoid than he had been, I was able to supervise and safely keep her with me for the number of years that she stayed in my home. When she left my care to spend some extended time with her family, she became pregnant and later gave birth to a cute baby boy. Not long afterwards, she returned alone to my home and I resumed caring for her. When the baby was about five months old, DYFS placed the baby into my home and I began caring for both mother and baby.

Within a couple weeks of coming to live in my home, I was alerted to the fact that the baby had some mental issues when I began noticing that he was making odd sounds and punching himself in his head and face. Had I not taken on the task of caring for the mentally challenged mother and her mentally challenged baby, I would've been able to keep her even longer than I did. However, I observed that she was becoming jealous of the attention that I gave to her baby. In a jealous rage she blurted out, "I'm going to kill you___! You get all the attention all the time!" Before I could shield the baby from the fury of his mother's jealousy, she lashed out as quick as lightening and punched her baby in the stomach as he lay cradled in my arms. With rapid-fire reflex to protect the baby from serious injury, I deflected some of the force of her blow by spinning my body away from the impact of her strike.

When the baby's mother realized that I was increasing my vigilance to ensure that she would not harm the baby, she then tried to harm herself. I was not ignoring her, but the baby demanded a lot of my time to properly care for him. Nevertheless, in an effort to get my attention, the mother used attention-seeking tactics like attempting to cut her wrists with my butter knife. The baby's birth date was the same as my brother, Bob's, so I took that to be a sign from the Lord that I should not discontinue caring for the baby, but that I should ask to have the mother placed elsewhere, where she could be cared for in a suitable nurturing environment. The Lord had prepared me and provided a place for me to serve those that He would put into my care. Caring for an adult whose mental status was severe, and caring for her child, who had mental and medical issues, was the beginning of my ministering to people outside the sphere of my family. I had to act on God's Word, believing and praying in faith as I'd never believed and prayed before. I kept myself prayerful, oftentimes on bended knees, because I realized that God wouldn't be pleased, if I didn't care for others the same as I had cared and done for my own family members.

> *Exodus 23:20 "...I send an Angel before thee, to keep thee in the way, and to bring thee into the place which I have prepared".*

A few years ago, after having dreamt about a tree that had praying hands hanging from the branches instead of leaves, I felt that the Holy Spirit was leading me to create a 'prayer tree'. Although I knew that I needed to pray always, during the good times and the bad times, I had become less fervent in my times of prayer; sometimes, only going through the motions. Oh, I prayed faithfully for my family members and for those whom I fostered and took care of. For quite some time I had lived by a verse of scripture that affirms that if I have iniquity in my heart when I pray, God won't hear me. I wanted the Lord to hear me whenever I prayed for my family and for those whom I loved.

Several of my family members had not yet come to the saving knowledge and acceptance of Jesus as their personal savior. Perhaps they may not have known how to seek God in prayer for themselves. I couldn't imagine not being able to get a prayer through to God on their behalf, if there ever was a matter of life or death facing them. If I willfully practiced sin in my life, God would not have heard and answered my prayers. So I bowed on my knees often to repent of sins that I was aware of and even for the sins that I was unaware of committing. I was continuously praying that God would remove every area of iniquity from my heart. *Ephesians 6:18* states that we ought to "*...pray in the Spirit on all occasions with all kinds of prayers and requests . . .*" So after that dream, I recognized that I wasn't praying as required in *2 Chronicles 7:14* that says *"If my people, which are called by my name, shall humble themselves, and pray, and seek my face, and turn from their wicked ways; then will I hear from heaven, and will forgive their sin, and will heal their land"*.

Immediately, following my dream, I went out and bought a large potted tree plant and began placing prayer requests on that potted plant. I told my children and those who came to visit me about the potted plant, and that I'd begun calling it my 'prayer tree'. I asked them to place their prayer request on a piece of paper, and paperclip it to a leaf on the tree. I assured them that I would pray especially for those requests throughout the year. I was reminded to pray all hours throughout the day by having the prayer tree in a highly visible area in my living room. Sometimes at night, when I found myself having a difficult time falling asleep, instead of turning on the T.V., I'd look at the prayer requests on the tree and begin praying for those needs. *Rev 22: 2* "*... and the leaves of the tree are for the healing of the nations".*

I shared about my prayer tree on my web-site, *www.vertiereid. com* and have since received many e-mails from people from all over the world. I respond to each person who gives me their e-mail address and I let them know that a copy of their prayer request is placed on my 'prayer tree'. When my prayer partners and I have our early morning prayers by phone, we pray for each request on the 'prayer tree'. It wasn't very long ago that I was on the verge of intervening in a matter involving a couple of my adult children. I was very distressed about the matter, because it pertained to some concerns I had about my grandchildren. While interceding one morning in prayer on behalf of others, I shared my apprehensions with my faithful prayer partners whether or not I should speak to my adult children about the problem. Within a matter of weeks, after we had lifted the matter up in prayer, the problem was resolved. It happened so quickly that I did not lose one pound while fasting and praying while deciding whether I should take my concerns to both of my children. *James 5:16 says "... Prayers offered by those who have God's approval are effective". (God's Word Translation)* I'm faithfully seeking the Lord to continue leading me to be effective in praying always.

When my children became adults, they moved away and started their own families. However, my husband and I still live on our same property. With us having a large in-ground swimming pool, summertime is a time of sharing and using everything, including our finances that the Lord has blessed us with, as a tool to witness to others. At any given time we have invited families and friends to come and enjoy a cookout at our home. Invitees are always welcomed to bring along guests. Because of God's generosity, we willingly extend ourselves and our resources to bless others, especially those who may be less fortunate than we are.

I remember reading in the Bible where Jesus was approached by a young ruler who asked, "What must I do to inherit eternal life?" Jesus cited the Commandments to that young man, who acknowledged that he had been keeping them from the days of his youth. The young man was extremely wealthy and focused on his earthy treasures. Jesus told him that if he sold all of his material possessions and distributed the money to the poor, he would have treasures in heaven; thus his focus would be shifted to heavenly treasures, and he would be free to follow Jesus. That probably wasn't exactly what that young man wanted to hear, so he went away sorrowful; not wanting to part with his earthly riches. He might have even been sorry that he had ever asked Jesus that question; for Jesus' answer was too much for that rich young ruler to handle.

1 Timothy 6: 17-19 Tell those who are rich in this age not to be arrogant and not to place their confidence in anything as uncertain as riches. Instead, let them place their confidence in God, who lavishly provides us with everything for our enjoyment. They are to do good, to be rich in good works, to be generous, and to share. By doing this they store up a treasure for themselves that is a good foundation for the future, so that they can keep their hold on the life that is real. (International Standard Version)

One cool evening, I went out to the church that I attended to meet a few women to pray and also to spend some quiet time with the Lord. At church, in a quiet corner, I knelt down and closed my eyes. Then I began crying out to the Lord in prayer for greater understanding concerning "repairers of the breach" and how that would apply to my life. The Holy Spirit began speaking to my innermost spirit with such urgency that I opened my eyes and stood to my feet. I looked around me, in the church sanctuary, and I questioned the Lord, "What am I looking for?" Before I could hardly get the words out of my mouth, I saw exactly what the Lord wanted me to see. The church seemed to be deteriorating right before my eyes. I saw peeling paint and cracks in the walls. The holes in the ceiling tiles stood out like black coals. Dirty windows with dirty curtains hung in the church, but I never really noticed it before. As the anointing rested heavily on me, a Scripture text came vividly to my mind, *"If my people which are called by my name, shall humble themselves, and pray, and seek my face, and turn from their wicked ways; then will I hear from heaven, and will forgive their sins, and will heal their land." (2 Chronicles 7:14)* Sin's offensiveness was vividly portrayed to me. The Holy Spirit enlightened me to see sin in peoples' lives as unappealing as I saw the church building with its peeling paint and cracks in the walls, its holes in the ceiling tiles, and its dirty windows with its soiled curtains. After trying in vain to explain what I had just experienced, to one of the women who also was in prayer at the church, I returned to my knees to pray. I sensed the warmth and tenderness of God's presence as I had many times before. I cried out of the depths of my spirit, "Lord, forgive us of our sins and heal our wretched land." I better understood that experience after I returned home from church. It was clear to me that God is preparing His servants to become "repairers of the breaches", to bring restoration to generations of people, whose lives are being destroyed due to the broken relationships in their families. Men, women, boys and girls, alike, all need the cleansing and healing that will come to them when they repent of their sins and accept Jesus as their own personal Savior. Only then, can they build a foundation that will last for generations to come; where love will be established and they will experience stability in their families. It is God's plan for mankind to be partakers of the divine nature.

> *2 Peter 1:4 Whereby are given unto us exceeding great and precious promises: that by these ye might be partakers of the divine nature, having escaped the corruption that is in the world through lust.*

I was filled with awe and admiration when I came to realize how much God really does love and care about me. When I finally grasped the Biblical concept of being fearfully and wonderfully made in His image, I also realized that God has a plan and purpose for my life. (*Psalm 139: 14*) I am not an accident in God's mind; He has a special plan for my life. In the beginning, I had a limited understanding of mankind being made in the image of God. (*Genesis 1: 26*)

As a child, I hadn't been taught much about the Bible, so I didn't know about the truths in the Scriptures that could be applied to me. I had never even heard anyone preaching the gospel, saying that I was fearfully and wonderfully made in God's image and likeness. I felt that I was made in the image of my parents even though I was raised by my mother. As I grew up, I saw her sinful lifestyle, which over a period of time began developing in my own life. When I became an adult, I was just like my mother. My mannerisms and behaviors reflected what I had witnessed in my mother's lifestyle. My life did not mirror the lifestyle of holiness that God requires.

For many years I lived in sin, not even realizing that I was designed to be more than who I had become. Since my mother did not have a relationship with the Lord when I was young, she failed to teach me His Word. She was unaware of the promises that God offers to all who keep His commandments. Had she had a relationship with the Lord, she also would have known that she was fearfully and wonderfully made. She would have portrayed the character of Christ, and His image of holiness would have been seen in her life. Then instead of me mimicking her sinful activities, I could have copied her lifestyle of holiness as she followed Christ.

However, as an adult I didn't know anything about God's love nor did I know that by following Jesus' example of love, I would be keeping His commandments. In ignorance, I satisfied the lusts of my flesh. I became involved in sinful activities that exposed my liver, lungs and my eyes to the deadly consequences of sin. From alcohol abuse, I could have developed cirrhosis of the liver. From cigarette smoking, my body could have been afflicted with the dreaded disease of emphysema. I could've contracted syphilis or gonorrhea, the sexually transmitted diseases (STD) that lead to visual blindness. I did not want my children to experience the deadly consequences of sin, so I was diligent to train them while they were young to rely on God's Word and to be obedient to its teachings. I taught my children about God's love, and prayed with them that they would continue to keep His commandments and not become involved in sinful activities.

> *Deuteronomy 6: 5-7 "…thou shalt love the Lord thy God with all thine heart, and with all thy soul, and with all thy might. And these words, which I command thee this day, shall be in thine heart: And thou shalt teach them diligently unto thy children, and shalt talk of them when thou sitteth in thine house, and when thou walkest by the way, and when thou liest down, and when thou risest up".*

God relies on parents to teach their children His laws. He expects parents to reinforce His principles. When we fail to live up to God's expectation of us as parents, by not training our children from their youth, we are in essence breaking our covenant of cooperation with

God. By teaching our children, in their early years, about God and their responsibility to obey Him, they will more than likely duplicate that training process to their children. They learn how to obey God's Word as they observe us obeying the Word of God. Our adherence to the principles of God's Word serves as a foundation of truth to help direct our children into the good that God has planned for their lives.

> *Jeremiah 29: 11—"I know the plans that I have for you, declares the LORD. They are plans for peace and not disaster, plans to give you a future filled with hope". (God's Word Translation)*

As long as parents are faithful to impart God's Word to their children at an early age, this firm foundation will carry over into the lives of their children and their children's children and to future generations.

> *Psalm 71: 17, 18 "O God, thou hast taught me from my youth: and hitherto have I declared thy wondrous works. Now also when I am old and greyheaded, O God, forsake me not; until I have shewed thy strength unto this generation, and thy power to every one that is to come".*

By not having been taught about the promises of obedience to God's Word, many children grow up hating what's right and good, and they engage in sinful activities that satisfy their youthful lusts. These children show no respect; not for God's law or for anyone else's authority. The times in which we live are very terrifying. Many of the youths in this generation have an affinity for violence.

> *Proverbs 30: 11-14 says, "There is a generation who put a curse on their father, and do not give a blessing to their mother. There is a generation who seem to themselves to be free from sin, but are not washed from their unclean ways. There is a generation, O how full of pride are their eyes! O how their brows*

> *are lifted up! There is a generation whose teeth are like swords, their strong teeth like knives, for the destruction of the poor from the earth, and of those who are in need from among men". (Bible in Basic English)*

Through the upcoming ministries of the "repairers of the breach," there is still hope for our children. History has a way of repeating itself. With that being so, what's happening now does not surprise me. It would only be surprising if the people of God don't respond to God's urgent call for them to take part in restoring the paths for our next generations.

> *Isaiah 58:12 "...they that shall be of thee shall build the old waste places: thou shalt raise up the foundations of many generations; and thou shalt be called, The repairer of the breach, The restorer of paths to dwell in".*

Children in foster care are placed in the homes of men and women who have become "repairers of the breach." They devote themselves to stand in the gap, some even from the day of the child's birth, serving as a substitute parent to these children who have been separated from their biological parents. All foster parents are expected to provide a loving and supportive environment in which these children can thrive. As one of the foster parents who have been called to be a "repairer of the breach," I have great faith that change is in the making.

All children need to be told that they are fearfully and wonderfully made in God's image, that God really loves them. Those who accept the ministry of foster parenting need to pass on the pure love of God to the children in their care. Embracing each child with unconditional love is necessary to stimulate a healthy sense of worth and security in that child. God's unconditional love is portrayed in *John 3:16*, which says "...God so loved the world, that he gave his only begotten Son, that whosoever believeth in him should not perish, but have everlasting life". His love stretches so far that it reaches above and beyond anything that could've ever been imagined to pardon the sins of the whole world. While the Scriptures make it clear that we do not have a license to practice sin, the Apostle John wrote that if we should fall into sin, there is a remedy for us.

> *1 John 2:1 "My little children, these things write I unto you, that ye sin not. And if any man sin, we have an advocate with the father, Jesus Christ the righteous:"*

God's parenting skills are reliable, and when we follow His guidelines we are sure to get good results. God is holy and even though He hates our sin, He loves us unconditionally. While rearing my own children, I learned the true meaning of unconditional love. Children, who have been separated from their biological parents, need that same unconditional love given to them by their foster parents. Giving love and hope to neglected and abused children is but a small sacrifice that we can make when compared to the supreme sacrifice that was made for us, that required the very life of God's only begotten Son.

CHAPTER FOUR

It's a God Thing

Giving hope and bringing restoration to children who are stuck in the "system," will be challenging. However, God uses men and women, like myself, who are dedicated to children who are in foster care. Our homes are opened to these orphaned or abandoned children many times without us knowing anything about them or their family history. Nevertheless, we are committed to get each child through the difficult times in their lives, regardless of what obstacles we might face. And believe you me; we are faced with many problems that would cause many people to say "Enough is enough! I can't do this any more!" We realize that we've been called by God to do this. Some of you who are reading this book have been called also. In other words, restoring the shattered lives of children is a "God Thing", and we are called to be involved.

Certain passages of Scripture come to my mind when I think about different people who had to overcome obstacles in their lives as they attempted to fulfill the various purposes that God was attempting to work out through their lives. Their stories are of special interest to me, because they show how similar the lives of ancient peoples were to modern day people. God spoke to Moses of His purpose to use him as a liberator. Moses had been drawn from attending to his father-in-law's sheep, to the burning bush where he was commissioned by God to lead the Israelites out of Egyptian bondage. Moses felt hesitant that the people would not be willing to accept his leadership without first knowing the name of the God who had given him that charge. So he desired to know the name of God that he might tell it to the people.

> *Exodus 4:1-4 "Moses answered and said, But, behold, they will not believe me, nor hearken unto my voice: for they will say, The LORD hath not appeared unto thee. And the LORD said unto him, What is in thine hand? And he said, A rod. And he said, cast it on the ground. And he cast it on the ground, and it became a serpent, and Moses fled from before it. And the LORD said unto Moses, Put forth thine hand, and take it by the tail. And he put forth his hand, and caught it, and it became a rod in his hand: that they might believe that the Lord God of their fathers, the God of Abraham, the God of Issac, and the God of Jacob, hath appeared unto thee".*

Moses was inexperienced; he had never led anyone to freedom, and initially felt that he was inadequate and unable to fulfill that call of God, as many of us may find ourselves today. When he was first summoned by God to go into Egypt to confront Pharaoh, I can only imagined that he was stricken with panic and apprehension.

> *Exodus 3:11 "Who am I that I should go to Pharaoh, and that I should bring the children of Israel out of Egypt?"* He also had a speech impediment, and didn't think that he was able to speak clearly enough to answer the call given to him by God. *Exodus 4:10 "…Moses said unto the LORD, O my Lord, I am not eloquent, neither heretofore, nor since thou hast spoken unto thy servant: but I am slow of speech, and of a slow tongue."*

Then after asking God for further proof of his commission, God told him to stretch out the shepherd's rod that he held in his hand. However insignificant Moses' shepherd's rod may have seemed to him to be, it became a powerful tool that displayed the mighty power of God first before Moses, then before the stubborn pharaoh of Egypt and the unbelieving Israelites. Even after being made aware of what could be done with the rod that he held in his hand, Moses still wasn't quite convinced that he was the man to do what God wanted done.

Forty years earlier, while he was prince in the palace of Egypt, Moses was emboldened to believe that he could fulfill God's purpose in his own power. But after being a fugitive and exiling himself, he spent forty years on the rough side of the mountain attending sheep. In his new life as shepherd, Moses had an ego-adjustment and was now humble enough that God could use him to free His people. I can relate to Moses quite well, because I've questioned God often because I lacked the wisdom needed to care for medically fragile children and adults who are challenged mentally. As Moses more-than-likely came to realize, he would not be operating in his own strength and wisdom, but in God's. I also realized that it's God's wisdom and strength that I depend on in everything that I do.

In the Bible book of Jeremiah it's recorded that God spoke to Jeremiah about the plan that He had for him even before his birth. God told him that he was sanctified and ordained to be a prophet to nations. After being told who he was and what he was called to do, Jeremiah, replied, "…*Ah, Lord God!…I cannot speak: for I am a child.*" (*Jeremiah 1: 6*) But before Jeremiah had been completely formed in his mother's womb, God had already ordained that Jeremiah would prophesy to the nations that had broken the covenant with Him. So when Jeremiah protested by saying that he was only a child, God's response to him made him know that God would give Jeremiah direction as to where he should go and what he should say. God said to him, "…*Say not, I am a child: for thou shalt go to all that I shall send thee, and whatsoever I command thee thou shalt speak*". (*Jeremiah 1: 7*) God equipped and prepared Jeremiah to go to the nations and preach His Words. He revealed to Jeremiah, even as a child, what he was called to do.

> *Jeremiah 1: 5 "Before I formed thee in the belly I knew thee; and before thou camest forth out of the womb I sanctified thee, and I ordained thee a prophet unto the nations".*

I'm encouraged when I read about the men and women who were equipped by God to carry out His plans. To fulfill God's plans for their lives, they had to exercise their faith in obedience to God. I know that I must exercise faith in God's plan for me. God expects me to move out in faith towards fulfilling His plan for my life as He reveals it to me step by step. All who desire to be used by God must humbly rely on God's Word as their source of direction. *Psalm 119:105 says, "Thy word is a lamp unto my feet, and a light unto my path."* Other Scripture clearly states that "it is impossible to please God without faith." All who accept Christ into their lives are commissioned to spread the gospel of His death, burial, and resurrection throughout the world; first to our own families, friends, and communities and around the world. Spreading the gospel to those who are not near us may pose the challenge to become involved by the giving of our finances to missions both far and near.

When Jeremiah was told by God that he had been set aside and ordained to be a prophet to the nations, Jeremiah hesitated. He told God that he was only a child. When God revealed what plans He had for Jeremiah, Jeremiah's response may have been motivated by fear and doubt that he would be able to fulfill God's commission for him. Anxiety flooded his soul when he realized that he would have to speak to not only one nation, but to the nations. I get uncomfortable when I have to speak in front of a few people; and absolutely petrified if I'm speaking to a large group.

Jeremiah was forewarned by God that he would face stiff opposition from not only the kings, princes, and priests of Judah, but also from the population in general. Jeremiah was told to not be intimidated by the stern faces of the people. He was to straighten up his back and stiffen his upper lip and speak all that God would command him to say. God was infusing Jeremiah with strength and courage. He would be undefeatable before his opponents. God gave Jeremiah the ultimate pep-talk of assurance of victory with words that could be paraphrased to say "They won't overpower you; I've got your back!"

Jeremiah 1:17-19 "Thou therefore gird up thy loins, and arise, and speak unto them all that I command thee: be not dismayed at their faces, lest I confound thee before them. For, behold, I have made thee this day a defenced city, and an iron pillar, and brazen walls against the whole land, against the kings of Judah, against the princes thereof, against the priests thereof, and against the people of the land. And they shall fight against thee; but they shall not prevail against thee; for I am with thee, saith the Lord, to deliver thee".

Moses and Jeremiah realized early that they needed to depend on God's strength and wisdom to begin and succeed in the tasks that God was commissioning them to do. My faith is challenged every day to depend on God's wisdom and strength for the out working of the plan that God has given me for my life. He prepares and equips me to do that which is totally impossible for me to do in my own limited wisdom and strength. The experiences that

I've read of men and women in the Bible, who were used by God to accomplish His purposes, revealed the importance of relying solely on God's wisdom and strength even as they endeavored to be obedient to His leadings. Because a person may or may not be a prominent, outstanding citizen in his or her community, does not mean that God could not or would not use them. If God can use an ass, He certainly can use a man, and sometimes He will even choose to use a woman.

There's not much mentioned in the Bible about whether or not Mary, the mother of Jesus, was a prominent, outstanding citizen in her community. However, it does say that she was a young virgin and she was one among many women who were summoned by God to fulfill His purposes. During Jesus' earthly ministry, He cast out seven demons from Mary Magdalene. After she had been set free, she remained one of His dedicated, loyal disciples. When that ministry came to its abrupt end with the cruel crucifixion, death and burial of Jesus, all of His followers were disillusioned and heartbroken. Three days later, Jesus was alive again, Mary Magdalene was the first one to see Him after He had risen from the dead, and He charged her to take a message to the rest of His disciples. She went to the rest of them and told them that Jesus said

> "...I ascend to my Father, and your father; and to my God and your God." (John 20: 17)

On another occasion during His earthly ministry, Jesus interacted with a Samaritan woman. He met her when she came to draw water from a well, and He took that opportunity to engage her in conversation. Among other things, He told her that she had had five husbands, and the man with whom she was presently living, was not her husband. She was amazed that He knew her past; she had never met Him before. In her excitement, she forgot why she had even gone to the well in the first place; leaving her water jar behind, she ran in haste back into the city, shouting, "Come see a man, who told me everything I did, he knew all about my past! (*John 4:28, 29*)

Similar to the Samaritan woman's encounter with Jesus, I, too, met the Savior. Like her, I had hidden issues in my past that others did not know about. There were secret sins and passions that I took care to guard really well. But I found out, that the whole of my life is exposed, like an opened book before the eyes of the Lord. The more I read the Word of God, the more I felt the need to unburden my sins before the Lord. I didn't fear what man could do to me if they found out about the secret sins I had held unto in my life. The Lord, He alone, has the keys of heaven and hell, life and death, and the Bible says that, *"He who keeps his sins secret will not do well; but one who is open about them, and gives them up, will get mercy". (Proverbs 28: 12) (Bible Basic English)* So, instead of concealing my evil thoughts and deeds, I repented of them and Jesus forgave me and cast my sins away from me "as far as the east is from the west . . ." *(Psalm 103:12)* Oh, what freedom! Like the Samaritan woman, I was so excited, I couldn't wait to tell others about my Savior and bring them to Him. I talked about Jesus to everyone I met. I read in the Bible about a certain sinner woman who learned that Jesus was dining at a certain Pharisee's house. She set out with a box of costly ointment and in humility she knelt and washed Jesus' feet with her tears and dried them with her hair. Then she tenderly kissed His feet and anointed them with the expensive ointment that she had brought along with her. With her faith, she put her love for Jesus into action. Jesus said to the woman, "Thy faith hath saved thee, go in peace". Like this woman, I too had many sins that Jesus, in His mercy, lovingly forgave. In grateful response, I'm offering my life wholly dedicated in His service. My love for Him is taking expression by my making Him top priority and foremost in my life. *(Luke 7:36-50)* Jesus paid the price for my redemption when He gave up His life for me; my life of service is all I can give to Him.

> *Ephesians 2:10 "God has made us what we are. He has created us in Christ Jesus to live lives filled with good works that he has prepared for us to do". (God's Word Translation)*

A great prophet of God, Elijah, had been commissioned to restore the hearts of the fathers and their children back towards each other. Through a mighty act of faith, Elijah also restored the hearts of the Israelites from worshipping the false god Baal, back towards the true and living God. Elijah challenged four hundred and fifty prophets of Baal to receive an answer from their god by sending fire down from heaven to consume the sacrifice that they had prepared for him. When no answer had come forth from their false god, Elijah began to call on the true God to consume his water-soaked sacrifice by sending fire from heaven. Within no time, Elijah's God answered by fire; licking up the water-drenched sacrifice and the water that had filled the trench that had been dug out at the base of the altar. The people stopped limping between two opinions; choosing to turn their hearts back to their God, they bowed themselves to the ground. Then the people were commanded, by Elijah, to immediately seize all the false prophets and drag them down to the brook Kishon and kill them there. Queen Jezebel's husband, King Ahab, had witnessed that confrontation. Returning back to the palace, he couldn't wait to tell her all that had been done, and how Elijah had slaughtered all her prophets. Angrily, she swore by the gods that his life would be snuffed out by the next day! When Elijah realized that Queen Jezebel had put out a contract on his life, he headed for the hills and hid himself away in a cave. Elijah was fearful for his life, and he thought of killing himself rather than facing Jezebel's brutal executioners. His fearfulness had forced out all thought of his superior God and how He had demonstrated His mighty power. Instead, Elijah's thoughts turned inwards, thinking only of his frail humanity and his inability to deliver himself from that angry woman. In spite of his weaknesses, God had used him and would continue to use him to further true worship.

By recognizing my mental and physical limitations, I realized the importance of depending on the wisdom and strength that God gives me. When I ask Him for it, I am equipped to serve others in meaningful ways. As I trust in God to fortify me, I am shielded from being overcome by paralyzing fear. God's Word instructs all of us that He "… hath not given us the spirit of fear; but of power, and of love, and of a sound mind." *(2 Timothy 1:7)*

When I've been fearful, it's been when I took my eyes off God. With my attention focused on the overwhelming circumstances that surrounded me, I felt gripped by my fear of not being able to control the situation. When I've been strengthened to perform valiantly, I rejoice greatly in my God. Many times, my victory over a certain situation will be followed by an even greater challenge in which I must continue to place my full confidence in God. At critical times, I've sometimes forgotten that the victory I experienced was because God had infused me with power. If I attempt to handle situations independently, I risk facing defeat and being held captive to fear.

With the confidence and boldness of a fearless lion, I've shared my faith in the Lord Jesus. Without fear, I've testified about what He's done in my life. On the other hand, there've been times when I was presented with opportunities to speak at seminars, on topics that I felt knowledgeable and qualified to speak on. But I was gripped by fear, right up to the moment that I was going up to the platform. My only thought was to renege on that engagement. My dominant thought was, "Oh, that the floor would open up to swallow me!" I would have welcomed it.

I related to Elijah's feelings of triumph when he prevailed mightily against the false prophets and I also related to the backlash of fear that afterwards attempted to drown him in self-pity when Jezebel sought to take his life. When his mind was darkened with clouds of fear, he did not remember that his victory had come because he had trusted and served the victorious God.

God had made my mouth and had given me a sound mind. But sometimes when I found myself in fearful situations, I forgot the many times that God had come to my rescue, and fear overpowered me, rendering me speechless. I felt insecure in my ability to make a coherent speech, and I dreaded the idea of babbling like an idiot before an audience. Had I trusted in God, all of my fears could have been conquered, and I would have been able to speak with boldness and confidence.

> *Luke 21:15 "For I will give you a mouth and wisdom, which all your adversaries shall not be able to gainsay nor resist."*

Job's fortunes and misfortunes are described in the Bible book that bears his name. Many times when bad things happen to us, we are tempted to place the blame on God rather than on the culprit. Sometimes we may not even know who or what has caused the problem. The devil was the instigator in all of Job's woes. God was so confident in Job's integrity and love for Him, that He was willing to prove that to the devil. God removed His protection from around Job's family and possessions. Job was not even aware of the existence of the devil, nor did Job have any idea that God had given the devil permission to afflict him. When Job was overwhelmed with grief and problem after problem, he thought that it might have been better if he had never been born. He expressed his feelings of extreme anguish and fear by saying that " ... *the thing which I greatly feared is come upon me, and that which I was afraid of is come unto me*". (Job 3: 25)

SMILE BANDAGES, REPAIRERS OF THE BREACH

Job was a rich man in the society in which he lived. He was enjoying his health, his wealth, his wife and his ten children when unexpected disaster struck. Suddenly, all ten of Job's children were killed in one fatal swoop; he suffered financial disaster with the loss of his flocks and herds, and lastly, his health took a nose dive. To make matters worse, three of his friends came to 'comfort' him during his time of grief. Sadly enough, they turned out to be 'false comforters'; they hurled false accusations against his spotless reputation of living a godly life. Although Job endured lengthy criticisms against himself from these friends, pride eventually rose up in him, forcing him to defend himself. Lastly, God intervened and declared His supreme wisdom, sovereignty and righteousness in all matters. Job was humbled by the realization that he lacked the wisdom and understanding to know what God was working behind the scenes. He was forced to confront the limitations of his humanity; he was no where around when God had formed and fashioned the universe out of nothing. When he had humbled himself, God used Job to pray for those same friends who had maligned his character. With Job's enlightened view of things, he felt no ill-will towards his friends for their erroneous charges. He realized that they also, in their ignorance, didn't know any more than he did. Humbled, God was able to use *Job* as the 'restorer and repairer of the breach' of friendship that had been brewing with undertones of doubt and mistrust.

Over the years, God gradually restored to Job all that he had lost, and he was again a very wealthy man. In his latter end, it could be said that God restored to Job all that the devil had snatched away from him. I too, suffered great, emotional pain with the deaths of my mother and all four of my brothers. When they all died young, cut off in the prime of their lives, I blamed God. At that time, I hadn't realized that the devil was the unseen villain behind the events that had led to the deaths of my loved ones. Centuries earlier, he was that 'thief' skillfully operating behind the scenes to cause Job's misfortunes. Later I learned about the mission of the enemy of all souls. It is his cruel intention to rob us of the abundant life that's offered to us by God. The Bible says of this enemy, "*The thief cometh not, but for to steal, and to kill, and to destroy: I am come that they might have life, and that they might have it more abundantly". (John 10:10)*

We all have sinned and have fallen short of God's glory. There are men and women mentioned in the Bible who although they lived ungodly lives, there came a moment of decision when they aligned themselves with God's purposes. Their choices placed them in line for God's mercy and salvation. Such was the experience of Rahab. She was the prostitute in the Bible town of Jericho who faithfully hid the two Israelite men who had been sent by Joshua to spy out the land. Instead of divulging their whereabouts and surrendering them, Rahab shielded them from being captured, and sent them safely back to the Israelites' camp. In Matthew's genealogy Rahab is listed as an ancestor of King David, who himself is an ancestor of our Savior, Jesus Christ. Like Rahab, I have pledged my allegiance to God's kingdom and through Jesus Christ, my eternal inheritance lies in His unmerited favor and abundant blessings.

Deborah was a woman who had many responsibilities. She was a godly woman, who was married and also a mother. Deborah was an anointed prophetess and judge. She was the fifth judge and the only female who served in the capacity of judge to Israel before the days of the kings. In her capacity as prophetess, Deborah reminded Barack that he had been summoned by God to gather a militia of ten thousand men to fight against the Canaanites; the pagan peoples who had banded together and oppressed Israel for twenty years. Barack's fearful response to her was "*… If thou wilt go with me, then I will go: but if thou wilt not go with me, then I will not go."* Deborah responded to his lack of confidence by saying, "*… I will surely go with thee: notwithstanding the journey that thou takest shall not be for thine honour; for the Lord shall sell Sisera into the hand of a woman. (Judges 4: 6-9)* Yes, Barak was weak in his faith at first, but he did muster up enough courage to go into the battle with Deborah leading the way. In spite of his shortcomings, Hebrews 11:32 lists him among other heroes of faith.

Deborah was so overjoyed with the victory that God had wrought through Barack and his men that she burst out in a victory song, 'The Song of Deborah'. Her song of praise, recorded in the

Bible, is said to be one of the finest examples of Hebrew poetry. Reading about Deborah, I was able to identify with her and I felt such admiration for her. Like Deborah I've been inspired to sing songs of victory to the Lord for the challenges He's helped me to overcome. The Holy Spirit revealed Deborah's exceptional character; in that she "stood in the gap" and worked along side of Barack by advising and encouraging him to lead the military into battle, instead of usurping authority over him and stepping into his position of authority.

Throughout biblical history, many women have had quite a few roles to play at the same time while they submitted their lives in humility to the Lord. As I summit myself to serving the Lord, I am wife, mother, grandmother, and the "mother figure" for the medically fragile children and mentally challenged adults in my care. Additionally, I have served in the vital capacity of "church mother", nurturing and caring for both the saints and those attending the church. In today's society, as I've fulfilled that essential role as "church mother," I've witnessed positive, spiritual growth in the lives of the church members as they've related to one another and to those coming into our church fellowship.

CHAPTER FIVE

I Learned the Hard Way

I experienced a few times of indecisiveness, where uncertainty was like a thick blanket covering me. It seemed as if I wasn't sure about what to do about anything any more. However, because I was the "church mother" in our ministry, I knew that I had to keep doing whatever service was required of me. It's the same thing that I'd done in past years while offering my service to God regardless of whatever else was going on. This was one of Satan's attacks, and I had to do whatever it took to get out from under his assaults. Time and time again, I cried unto the Lord, asking "why are all these things happening, and what am I supposed to do about it". This spirit of indecision was very confusing to me. I read in the Bible that a double-minded person was unstable in all of their ways. I was afraid that, that had begun happening to me.

    I raised my children to honor God, and I believed that was pleasing to Him. When He gave me somebody else's children to teach about His principles, I assumed God was pleased that I was using the talents He'd given to me. I'm pleased when I think about how the Lord had given me the ability to be not only a good mother to my children, but also a good foster mother. I

felt like I was in the "third heaven" when He called me to serve as the "Mother" of a church.

    I received many rewards from the Lord while mothering my children and the children whom I fostered. Over the years He told me many things, but the one thing that I remember, as if it was yesterday, was that if I raised my children to love and respect me as their mother while they are young, they would respect Him as their God as they matured to adulthood. They did it too. I've always received the utmost respect from them. My children even call me "blessed" just like it's written in the Bible book of Proverbs, chapter 31 and verse 28 which says "Her children shall arise up, and call her blessed; her husband also, and he praiseth her."

After becoming the "Mother" of the church and mothering the church members for more then ten years, I've received much love and admiration from them. I cried out to the Lord on their behalf for godly wisdom to instruct them just like I had done while I was rearing my own children. By feeling close to the church members and having a genuine interest in their lives, we experienced a mutually rewarding relationship. Many times the members in the church told me that I blessed their lives; they certainly have been a blessing in mine. I enjoyed serving them in the capacity as "church mother" and at the same time rendering my service to the Lord.

When a spirit of restlessness hung like a shadow over me, I didn't know what to do or where to go. When I prayed for direction, God elevated me from a place of doing something that I felt comfortable doing, to doing something that was more challenging and more than I could've ever imagined that I could do.

As I pondered the Scriptures, I saw that God had at one time in the past used a jackass to cause a man to be still, thus sparing the man's life. When I encountered a certain unexpected situation, and "I felt stuck", I wondered what catalyst God would use to get me going again in the right direction. I prayed that God would intervene, even if it meant using extreme measures in my life, to further promote the work of the church.

Even if we are in a place where we might feel very familiar and comfortable, that's no guarantee that we're in the ministry that God intends for us to stay in. We might be comfortable doing something that we've been doing for years and not even recognize when we're being summoned by God to leave for a different assignment. Even Abraham was called to leave the place of his roots, Ur of the Chaldees.

(Genesis 11:31) He had been living in his father's house amongst his pagan family, when he was told by God that it was time for him to get out and leave that country. God told Abraham that He would lead him to the land in which He will make him to be a great nation, and not only would he have a great name, but that he would be blessed to be a blessing.

A former pastor of mine, the late Dr. Donald Womack, through his preaching instilled in me the importance of having a good name and being blessed of the Lord. Abraham's name is known throughout history by his faith and trust in God; the legacy of his blessings is passed down through many generations. Through faith and by trusting in God's Word, I'm blessed through the blessings of Abraham.

The teachings of God's Word were preached to me through the late Dr. Donald Womack. They continue to encourage and motivate me to be more Christ-like in order to win souls for the Kingdom. His teachings of faith are yet being taught in a Bible-based Institute that was started by him. The late Dr. Donald Womack's dependence on God was demonstrated by the life that he lived. His faith was seen by his accomplishments: his audio tapes and the books he wrote that were distributed in the United States and throughout the world. In one of his sermons, he preached that a blessed man is a man who is able to meet the needs of mankind regardless of what their needs might be. I cherished all of his many sermons, however, the one that he preached about a blessed man, will forever be one of my favorite sermons. After the late Dr. Donald Womack preached that particular sermon, I sought after God as I had never sought after Him before. I wanted to be a blessed person and be able to meet the needs of mankind. I learned that mankind's needs would only be met, as were my needs met, by accepting Jesus as my personal Savior and Lord. I allowed the Holy Spirit to prepare my life so that I would be able to stand in the gap to reach others through sharing the gospel.

When one has been operating in the church in a certain capacity, and God reveals a new dimension of that calling, it may be necessary to reach out in faith to grab hold of that expanded vision. God's plan for you to leave your present environment and enlarge your territory may not always be understood by others. Reaching for a higher level of commitment in God's service is usually not self-motivated. When I left my place of comfort, endeavoring to fulfill what God had placed on my heart, I had to depend on God to bring the vision into reality. When you move into new territory, you will be facing more challenges with God than you could've ever imagined. Going through uncharted territory, with God's leading, is proving more fruitful and rewarding to me than if I had remained stagnant in my previous comfort zone.

While I'd been ministering in the capacity as "church mother", I felt that God was preparing me for a ministry that would eventually take me outside the realm of the local church's ministry. When it came time for me to part company with the church that I had been associating with, I had become so comfortable that I didn't want to leave. As Jonah, in the Bible, had resisted doing what God had told him to do, I resisted making the change that God was trying to lead me to make as I stubbornly held on to what God was trying to get me to release. In disobedience Jonah chose to flee in the opposite direction. In my disobedience, I wanted to stay planted where I already was. Some unfortunate events unfolded before I finally felt a release in my spirit to leave that ministry. When I say that I learned my lesson the hard way, you can believe me, it was a devastating lesson that I needed to learn.

Although I was clueless regarding just where I was supposed to go, I knew that I was supposed to follow God's leading. Abraham, who had lived so many centuries ago, was just as clueless as to where God was going to lead him. He also had to step out in faith to follow God's leading. My natural mind raced to and fro trying to figure out what my next move should be. But to the rescue came the Spirit of God who brought calmness to the flurry of ideas and plans that tried to rob me of God's peace. God's Word gently reminded me, *"Trust the LORD with all your heart, and do not rely on your own understanding. In all your ways acknowledge him, and he will make your paths smooth"*. *(Proverbs 3:5, 6,)(God's Word Translation)*

We all suffered emotional loss when the pastor unexpectedly and suddenly left our church. After having just been abandoned by a pastor who had been the shepherd over us for more than ten years, we were as lost sheep wandering in the pasture. For months we were a cluster of people without a leader, so many people chose to fellowship elsewhere during that unfortunate period. The board and the members did everything that we could, determined not to let our church doors close. We became known as the 'little church who could' because we just wouldn't give up.

> *Psalm 75:6, 7 For promotion cometh not from the east, nor from the west, nor from the south. But God is the judge: he putteth down one, and setteth up another.*

In time God placed a "new pastor" to shepherd our congregation. He preached sermons that were full of God's power and anointing. Healing and restoration came forth through his messages; not only for the church members, but for all of the people who came to fellowship with us. Our board members had begun managing everything before the arrival of the "new pastor". There were only a few of us board members, but we worked busily. We were Jesus' dedicated disciples. The ones who stayed behind at the church did more than their share to get things back on track, once the former pastor, church secretary, deacons, and praise and worship leader had all gone. We encouraged one another while continuing our fellowship meetings at the church. With the presence of the Holy Spirit in our midst at our services, we were blessed mightily. There was so much harmony amongst us. If there was anyone who didn't understand the words stated in the Bible concerning unity amongst brethren, they could have certainly seen it through us. For months, the church members and the board of administrators were all in one accord. What happened next, after the installation of our 'new pastor', almost shook the living daylights out of me.

The "new pastor", who had been one of the two interim ministers, was 'voted in' to be the shepherd over our ministry. Everyone seemed to be so excited to have a pastor over our church again. I think all of us had high hopes and expected things to fall into place right away. Shortly after the installation service for the 'new pastor', trouble seemed to be coming from everywhere. The usually calm and tolerant atmosphere of the administrative board meetings almost immediately became charged with chaos and confusion. The ensuing spirit of unrest quickly contaminated the general congregation and soon there were pockets of hot sparks of bitter hurtful words and haughty attitudes being paraded amongst our church members. The Holy Spirit of God was needed to extinguish the smoldering embers of impatience and distrust that threatened to erupt into full-blown flames. The apostle Paul warned against this situation in Galatians 5:15-" ... if ye bite and devour one another, take heed that ye be not consumed one of another." Had I not been right in the midst of it all, I might have been able to detect Satan's subtle influence to disrupt the harmony of our little group.

Even before my former pastor had deserted the church, the Holy Spirit had begun pressing in my spirit that my time of service as 'church mother' was coming to an end and that I would be leaving that body of believers to expand my ministerial calling as evangelist. A few months before the "new pastor" had been installed at our church, again I sensed that the Lord was summoning me to expand the territory of my ministry.

Although there were more than a few indications that a significant change was coming for me, I refused to acknowledge it. The 'new pastor' asked a woman who had recently joined our fellowship to serve as 'church mother'. Previously he had made a statement to me that he'd never before shepherded over a ministry that had a 'church mother'. Yet, now he wanted to have two church mothers. The eyes of my understanding should have been opened to the message that the Holy Spirit had been trying to impart to me, but they weren't. Nevertheless, this godly woman and I bonded immediately, and were like sisters in Zion. We worked so well together offering our services to the Lord; it was as if we'd known one another all of our lives.

Another signal that passed by me unheeded, was when the 'new pastor' prophesied during one of his sermons that the Lord was raising up people in our church to do great and mighty things, like being an author. This confirmation in the new pastor's preaching should have really convinced me that it was the Lord's timing for me to move on; that the Holy Spirit was releasing me from a ministry that I'd been involved in for more than ten years.

Although my ears had perked up, my inner understanding remained dull. I'd already written my first book and I was in the process of writing the second one. The titles of these two books were based on the sermons that I'd preached on two different occasions to the congregation while I was under my former pastor. As 'church mother', I was called on often to minister to the congregation. On the other hand, the 'new pastor' wasn't releasing anyone to share in the ministering of the gospel. The assistant pastor was rarely given an opportunity to bring forth the Word of God during church services, while other credentialed ministers in our church were generally overlooked for ministerial preaching opportunities. However, he did extend preaching opportunities to his wife, though they were few and far between.

I was wrong to think that the church wouldn't survive without me. I had busied myself in the ministry by doing a little of everything; hemming curtains, vacuuming floors, cooking and serving church dinners, and I continued visiting the senior citizens in the nursing homes. I was so engaged in offering my services as 'church mother' to the Lord that it never crossed my mind that my ministry with that church would ever come to an end. There's an old wives' tale that I remember hearing, which says 'if parents want to raise their children without ruin, they must kill the grandmother.' I understand the meaning of that saying now that I'm a natural grandmother. Grandmothers, not all of them, usually spoil their grandchildren rotten by giving in to their grandchildren's cries.

Grandmothers very seldom do they use the same rod of correction on their grandchildren that they used while rearing their own children. When my grandchildren visit with me, I'm not as strict in disciplining them as I had been with my own children when they had misbehaved. I hardly ever gave in to the cries of my children, yet, when my grandchildren are around me, I allow them to get away with much more than I had allowed my children to get away with when they were young. If I had stayed on at the church for the new generation of people coming into that fellowship, I could have been likened to a church's 'grandmother'. My days had run out for 'mothering' in that church's ministry.

God didn't intend for me to stay any longer with that church fellowship, but when I took it upon myself to stay, Satan 'wreaked havoc' on my nerves. As Job's three friends had called his character into question, my 'new pastor' had taken it upon himself to call my character into question. Among other things, he falsely accused me of being an "outright liar". That false charge was hurled, within the hearing of others, to slander and damage my reputation of being a truthful, God-fearing woman. Unwittingly, Satan used my 'new pastor' to wage an assault attack on my Christian character. That surprise attack was like an ambush; it was forcefully aimed to 'steal' my good name, 'destroy' my Christian testimony and to utterly 'kill' my influence in that ministry. That awful experience left me emotionally and physically drained.

When our 'new pastor' began to sit in on our monthly administrative board meetings, I began to sense the undercurrent of a developing power struggle. Sometimes suggestions were voiced that conflicted with his opinions to correct whatever new problem had arisen since the last board meeting. Our 'new pastor' had not yet become familiar with the personalities of those who sat on the board. Perhaps, as a newcomer, he may have felt especially intimidated by my presence as the 'mother' of the church. My opinions were highly regarded by those who knew me for many years; those opinions weren't always right, but I was always respected.

> *1Thessalonians 5: 12, 13…we beseech you, brethren, to know them which labour among you, and are over you in the Lord, and admonish you; And to esteem them very highly in love for their work's sake. And be at peace among yourselves.*

My 'former pastor' had appointed me as an advisor in spiritual matters and in church matters in particular. I sat on the church's administrative board, and during our monthly board meetings, church business and church affairs were discussed. All board members freely shared their opinions concerning biblical doctrine and church etiquette. We were all responsible to make suggestions or to call into question anyone who had a position of responsibility in the church, whose behavior had become inappropriate. Then upon the pastor's recommendation, we could ask the offending person to step down from his or her leadership position in the ministry until such time as their behavior was again Christ-like.

My 'new pastor' did not highly esteem me for my work's sake; he had not gotten to know me. Before he came, we had years of peace and harmony in our board meetings. When the devil, working through our 'new pastor', sought to swallow up my influence within that fellowship, by calling me a liar, that malevolent incident convinced me that my time of serving there as 'church mother' had come to its end. When the devil had lifted his ugly head with strife, contention, and name callings, peace walked out the door and harmony jumped out the window; and I realized, without a shadow of a doubt, that I had to be obedient and follow God's leading.

CHAPTER SIX

Can You Hear Me Now?

"Yes, Lord, I hear You now!" It had finally sunk into my heart that God had been speaking to me, but my spiritual ears had not been tuned in to what He had been saying. Although I had turned a deaf ear to His voice, how could I have missed the visible signs that were right in front of my eyes? I knew that my steps had been ordered by the Lord while I had been serving Him in the capacity of 'church mother'. I felt needed as the 'church mother,' so I convinced myself that that was the ministry position that I was to remain in. "Oh God, what kind of mess have I gotten myself into, because of my disobedience and refusal to continue following Your leading?"

About nine months after our 'former pastor' deserted the church, we chose one of the two 'interim ministers' to be the shepherd leader of our ministry. Our administrative board now included Prophetess Lynn Smith, the 'new pastor' and his wife, me, and Deacon Brian Walton. Prophetess Lynn Smith had served for quite a few years alongside our 'former pastor'. Her spiritual insight and wisdom were vital during the church's transitional period of recovering from the deterioration that had occurred due to the former pastor's indiscretions that had left many demoralized. Our board meetings had grown to be so frustrating and tiresome, leading up to the emotionally explosive outbursts that took place in the final board meeting that I had attended. The ending of that board meeting was one of the most humiliating occurrences I'd ever experienced.

I'd never been so embarrassed in the whole time that I'd been in the church. Had I been listening more closely to God, all of this could have been avoided. I knew that the Lord had been trying to release me from serving Him as the 'church mother' for awhile. Had I known that it would have ended like this, in a shouting match, I would have left even before my former pastor ran off.

Before officially being 'voted in' as the 'new pastor', he was informed of what he could and could not do as the church's interim pastor. However, after being installed as the 'new pastor', he often took the liberty to make decisions without first consulting with the board. Then he made the concession that the board members were welcome to discuss the decision that he had already made. In fact, he said that he invited our opinions and criticisms; yet when they were offered, he became highly defensive.

It was difficult for pastor's wife to disagree with her husband. Noticeably, after she became a board member, pastor's wife had a difficult time siding with other board members as they were trying to deal with important issues and suggestions that her husband was vigorously opposing or trying to ignore. Regrettably, pastor's wife seemed partial and protective towards her husband's authority in the church. It was hard for her to uphold and offer support to the general consensus of the majority of the board members who endeavored to be led by the wisdom of God when making decisions that affected the whole church.

I believe that a wife should be submissive to her husband in their own family matters. However, it is highly important that she remain impartial, open, and obedient to God's leading in matters affecting the church's body of believers. It is of utmost importance that when God calls someone into ministry, that he or she be submissive to the Lord, first and foremost. It is noted in *1 Corinthians 7: 34* that *"…An unmarried woman or virgin is concerned about the Lord's affairs: Her aim is to be devoted to the Lord in both body and spirit. But a married woman is concerned about the affairs of this world-how she can please her husband." (New American Standard Bible)* Shortly after I became his wife, my own husband acknowledged that my desires were to serve the Lord whole-heartedly. He recognized that I was responsible to fulfill my duties in the ministry that God had assigned to me. He freely released me to serve as a servant of the Lord, rather than insisting that I serve him first like a traditional wife would be expected to do. My husband understood that I would be blessed in my obedience to the Lord and he granted me the freedom to serve God. I often told him that he would be blessed and benefit from all of the blessings that the Lord would bestow on me.

I offered wholehearted service to the Lord; being diligent in the ministry that the Lord had entrusted to me, and also taking care of my household responsibilities. As others acknowledged my accomplishments, they also realized my husband's sacrifices and generosity in allowing me to serve the Lord in reaching out to help others in our community. Those who visited me and my husband often spoke about the blessings that the Lord had bestowed upon our lives. I am a wife who not only strives to please God in serving Him, but by putting God first, I'm learning how to be a good wife for my husband.

> *Proverbs 31: 10-12 "A wife of noble character who can find her? She is worth far more than rubies. Her husband has full confidence in her and lacks nothing of value. She brings him good, not harm, all the days of her life." (New International Version)*

The Lord blessed my husband and me with four lovable children. While they were young, I nurtured and mothered them; training them in the ways of the Lord. It was during those years, as I was bringing up my children, that God began preparing me for the ministry of serving as 'church mother'. God had elevated my former pastor from being a 'youth minister' in the church that he had attended, to being a pastor in a small church of his own. I was licensed to be an evangelist, before I was ever asked to be a 'church mother'. However, when I was asked by my 'former pastor' to come and assist him in the ministry as the 'mother of the church', I didn't think that being a 'church mother' was what I was called to be. Yet, being 'church mother' later proved to be one of the most fulfilling and rewarding, ministry assignments that God could have ever called me to fulfill.

Zechariah 4:10 "For who hath despised the day of small things? . . ."

When I shared with one of my close friends that I was asked to be the 'mother of the church', it didn't surprise me when she said, "What, a mother of the church! You are not that old, Sister Reid". She thought it was funny and began to laugh. Immediately, I regretted having shared with my friend that the young preacher had asked me to be the 'church mother' of his young church. My friend and I were only a year and a few months apart, but I actually looked younger than she did. She was at least one hundred and fifty pounds overweight, causing her to look much older. She looked like she was somebody's 'church mother'!

I knew that the young preacher didn't think of me as a senior citizen. He'd admired the relationship that I had with my children. I was certain that he thought that I was a godly woman and mother who would enhance his ministry. My teenage daughters had become involved in the youth services held at the church where he had been the youth minister, so I started attending the church services along with them. When the youth minister decided to be a pastor, having his own church, he asked me to come alongside him as 'church mother' to help him. I didn't know very much about 'mothering' a church, but I knew that 'church mothers' were given recognition and much respect. My own mother died in her late forties. For two years, prior to her death, she served as 'church mother'. She was an attractive, young-looking, godly woman.

I'd always believed that a 'church mother' was a woman of wisdom, who prayed for her pastor and the church members. My mother had been a prayer warrior. My friend and I had both started our Christian walks when we were younger and inexperienced in the faith. We made many unwise decisions, but as I matured in the faith, I became wiser. If she had told me that she was asked to be a 'church mother', I might have thought it was funny too. So, I wasn't surprised that my friend thought that 'church mothers' were seniors.

> *Hebrews 5:13, 14 All those who live on milk lack the experience to talk about what is right. They are still babies. However, solid food is for mature people, whose minds are trained by practice to know the difference between good and evil. (God's Word Translation)*

I realized that 'mothering' church members, under that young preacher, was an honorable position in the ministry, so, I accepted that position. I sought the Lord and He instructed me how to be a good and gracious 'church mother'. Those years of being a 'church mother' have given me a wealth of experiences to write about.

My own mother had been much younger when she had become a 'mother of the church' than I was when I became a 'mother of the church'. She was one of the most dedicated 'church mothers' that I've ever known. Her motherly love, nurturing, and deeds of kindness towards the members in the church, were warmly received. My mother treated everyone, both inside and outside of her church fellowship, as if they were her own children. They loved and honored her like children are told to do in the Bible. My mother was affectionately known as 'Mother Pringle'.

I committed myself to serve the Lord as the 'church mother' and embraced its members with deeds of love as if they were my very own children. I followed the pattern of love that I saw in my mother's ministry as a 'church mother' towards her church family and those she came in contact with. I have also received love and respect from those in my own church fellowship and from those who know me. They all call me 'Mother Reid'.

The young pastor and I, as the 'church mother', became as one having the same mind in the things of the Lord in the ministry. He accepted the wisdom of my suggestions, and as he submitted himself to the guidance of the Holy Spirit, he was able to discern that what I'd spoken to him had been given to me from the Lord. Spiritual principles are non-negotiable. We didn't always agree on minor, non-biblical issues; but we were always united when it came to upholding the standard of righteousness as set forth in the Bible.

> *1 Cor 1:10 'Now I beseech you, brethren, by the name of our Lord Jesus Christ, that ye all speak the same thing, and that there be no divisions among you; but that ye be perfectly joined together in the same mind and in the same judgment".*

Just as I prayed for my own children, I prayed much for those under the ministry of my former pastor. In love, I endeavored to give them good, sound advice from the Word of God. Serving as church mother under that young preacher's ministry was an awesome experience for me. The pastor and I were a help one to another when he recognized, just as my husband had, that I was responsible to God to fulfill my duties in the ministry that God had called me to do. I submitted my life to God and for years while serving in that church under the ministry of my former pastor. Through the guidance of the Holy Spirit growth was recognized, not only in me, but in the lives of all who fellowshipped there.

When God began summoning me for another assignment, I didn't realize it until different pieces began to fall into place. The Holy Spirit had been beckoning me, for some time, to spend more time with the nursing home ministry, even before my former pastor had left the church. Additionally, when the 'new pastor' installed another 'mother of the church' along with me, it appeared to me that my service was no longer needed. The final 'straw that broke the camel's back' was when, in a meeting with the 'new pastor', I expressed the inappropriateness of my foster child participating in the praise dance ministry at the church since her conduct was not above reproach. The 'new pastor' proceeded to belittle my concerns at that time. That's when I considered leaving the ministry, but I stayed on for awhile longer. After some time, I eventually handed in my letter of resignation because I felt that we no longer shared the same mind and the same judgment on important spiritual principles. The following is the letter that I submitted:

Pastor *(new pastor)* and Rev. *(his wife)*

Believe it or not, this is one of the hardest things I've had to do in a long time. With deepest regrets, I must resign from this fellowship ministry. I honestly can't say that I know what I will be doing in the near future, because at this particular time I really don't know.

I will not drag this out any longer than necessary for me to explain to you why I feel that it is time for me to leave. Pastor, I hope this won't come across as if I don't respect you and your ability of knowing how to minister to your congregation, because that is not the impression that I want to leave with you or anyone else.

It might just be me and my old fashioned ideas that the Holiness of God must be seen in the lives of those who are called upon to minister in God's sanctuary. Pastor, you know my feelings about the dance ministry, and because of those feelings I can't sit under this ministry any longer. I am not involved in any thing that will suffer by my leaving, so I will quietly wean from all duties in the ministry.

When Rev. *(his wife)* suggested I take over that ministry, you said that you did not want me to do it; that was the best thing that could have happened. I can't say for sure how I would have handled such a touchy subject of whether someone should be allowed to usher the presence of God through ministering in dance, through preaching the Word or any other aspects of ministry if they still lived with their boyfriend. It is hard enough for me to explain to my dancers the importance of living holy if the other dancers are not doing the same.

I will continue with the duties in the ministry that I am a part of through the end of March 2008; I will then return my keys to the board. WOW! I can't believe that I have been in *(church)* all these years. I must say that it has been an experience that I will treasure and keep in my memories.

(Church) you will forever be in my prayers,

Evangelist, Mother Vertie Reid

I've read and reread that letter, which I had submitted to 'my new pastor', just to see if what I'd written caused the unwarranted outburst. I'd never been in such a hostile disagreement, with such an angry exchange of words with anyone, as had occurred in the final board meeting that I had attended. My foster daughter was eighteen years old and no longer living at home with me. I'd begun to teach the younger youths and they looked up to the older youths as role models. So, as soon as one of the youngsters in my dance group brought to my attention that my foster daughter and her boyfriend were living together, I approached the pastor with the hope that he would uphold the standard of holiness that I was already teaching diligently to the young people. Since I was not in charge of the older youth's dance ministry, it wasn't my place to ask her to step down from it. However, as her pastor, he had authority over both dance ministries, and he could have asked her to step down if her lifestyle was contrary to biblical standards. When the pastor began to verbally attack me, by maligning my good name, at first, I was so stunned that I was speechless. Expecting his wife to come to my defense or to do something that would let him know that he was grossly out of order, I turned my head towards her. The whole time I was being verbally abused and slandered, she kept her head bowed, perhaps, she was praying. Deacon Brian was desperately trying to interrupt to say something, but he couldn't get a word in edgewise. It was as if he was being deliberately ignored by the 'new pastor', so he couldn't speak in my defense if he wanted to. As Prophetess Lynn looked on in disbelief and horror, I watched the color drain from her face. Since becoming a Christian, I've never been at a loss for words, but for a moment, 'the cat had my tongue'. Usually if someone said something to me in an abrasive manner, my answer would boomerang right back just as sharply. However, this was my pastor and I didn't know exactly how I should challenge his negative, untruthful charges. Without being provoked, I would've never blurted out, "You are a liar!" but I was provoked. Who would've ever thought that I'd be in such a war of words with a 'man of God'?

It was months later, after reading that letter that I understood that it wasn't the letter that had upset the 'new pastor'. The letter infuriated the pastor and his reaction was the catalyst that got my attention and got me thinking on what God had been saying to me all along. In the Bible, when Jonah hadn't followed God's leading, he was cast overboard and landed in the angry waters before being quickly swallowed into the belly of a huge fish. When I hadn't followed God's earlier leading, I was viciously attacked and I felt like a wounded outcast. In the past, I would have said to someone who had offended me, "You can bet your sweet little life that I won't lose any sleep over anything that you've said". But this particular drama scene, that had taken place in the board meeting, was like a dreadful nightmare, and I can say with all honesty that I didn't sleep at all that night. Having Prophetess Lynn Smith on the church board and in attendance at that fateful meeting, she was able to see how distressed and upset I was. I put up a good front, but, I was crushed, and Prophetess Lynn Smith gave me emotional support in the days, weeks, and months that followed.

The 'new pastor' didn't calm down, until he ran out of words. After he had unburdened himself of all of the pent up anger and frustration that he must have been feeling towards me, he apologized for telling me off and asked for my forgiveness. He then said to everyone on the board, that he thought that his old ways were so far behind him that he never anticipated becoming so frustrated that his old nature would rise up again. He continued apologizing and even though I forgave him, I knew that I could not easily forget it.

The 'new pastor' tried telling us the reason for his frustration, and what part he felt that we played in him being 'pushed to the edge'. At that point, I had begun to lose all interest in what he was saying. I really thought his explanation was a cop-out, but I did tell him that had he been addressing those problems with the board members all along, he could have avoided the big blowout that had just occurred. We continued our board meeting for another ten minutes or so. Someone prayed. We all scattered; I went home.

During those next few days, my phone rang almost non-stop. Thankfully, it was Prophetess Lynn Smith checking in on me almost every hour. Only God knows how much I needed her reassurance that I had not behaved in a manner that was contrary to how one would have acted if placed in a similar situation. She had been an eye-witness to my awful encounter with the pastor. Had she not continued calling me to give me support and encouragement, I doubt very much that I would have continued to attend the church services until the day that my resignation was scheduled to take effect.

Clearly, God was making it known to me that He had a new direction of expansion for my nursing home ministry. I was to be operating, to a fuller extent, beyond the confines of that fellowship. My disobedience and reluctance to leave the church, when God had first placed it in my heart, had far-reaching effects. The unpleasant incident at that board meeting was a direct repercussion of my slowness to be obedient. Ancient Jonah's slow obedience caused the ship's crew to be in danger of drowning in the storm that rose up suddenly at sea. The ship's crew frantically threw everything overboard, in efforts to stay afloat. Jonah pleaded with them to throw him overboard, so that they wouldn't have to experience the wrath of God on his account. Had Jonah obeyed sooner, he could have spared himself and others much hardship and loss, because he eventually obeyed. Neither Deacon Brian Walton, nor Prophetess Lynn Smith would have dared to throw me, the 'church's mother', overboard, even if I had pleaded with them to do so. Both of them upheld me, as my faithful armor bearers in prayer, and they continued to remind me of my faithful years of service and the good reputation that I had earned throughout my time at the church. It's just like what the Bible says in *Proverbs 22:1* "A good name is more to be desired than great wealth, and to be respected is better than silver and gold."

Within the week before my resignation would be taking effect, the pastor's wife started calling and visiting me at my home, attempting to persuade me to change my mind about leaving the church. On one of her visits I told her that she might want me to stay at the church, but that I was certain that her husband didn't feel the same way. She didn't deny that sentiment. I had no doubts that I had overstayed my welcome when her husband had angrily shouted at the top of his voice, "Mother Reid, I accept your resignation!"

From conversations shared with the pastor's wife, I knew her views on being a 'submitted wife'. It must have been difficult for her to oppose her husband by asking me to stay. I truly believe that the pastor's wife is an anointed vessel of God. In my opinion, I regret that she was not as committed to God, as she was submitted to her husband. As Christians, we remain friends and continue to support one another in prayer. While writing my thoughts on how devoted a pastor's wife should be to her husband, a very familiar passage from the Bible flashed before me.

> *1 Samuel 25: 2-38… "A certain man in Maon, who had property there at Carmel, was very wealthy. He had a thousand goats and three thousand sheep, which he was shearing in Carmel. His name was Nabal and his wife's name was Abigail. She was an intelligent and beautiful woman, but her husband, a Calebite, was surly and mean in his dealings.*
>
> *While David was in the desert, he heard that Nabal was shearing sheep. So he sent ten young men and said to them, "Go up to Nabal at Carmel and greet him in my name. Say to him: 'Long life to you! Good health to you and your household! And good health to all that is yours!*
>
> *"'Now I hear that it is sheep-shearing time. When your shepherds were with us, we did not mistreat them, and the whole time they were at Carmel nothing of theirs was missing. Ask your own servants and they will tell you. Therefore be favorable toward my young men, since we come at a*

festive time. Please give your servants and your son David whatever you can find for them.'"

When David's men arrived, they gave Nabal this message in David's name. Then they waited.

Nabal answered David's servants, "Who is this David? Who is this son of Jesse? Many servants are breaking away from their masters these days. Why should I take my bread and water, and the meat I have slaughtered for my shearers, and give it to men coming from who knows where?" David's men turned around and went back. When they arrived, they reported every word. David said to his men, "Put on your swords!" So they put on their swords, and David put on his. About four hundred men went up with David, while two hundred stayed with the supplies.

One of the servants told Nabal's wife Abigail: "David sent messengers from the desert to give our master his greetings, but he hurled insults at them. Yet these men were very good to us. They did not mistreat us, and the whole time we were out in the fields near them nothing was missing. Night and day they were a wall around us all the time we were herding our sheep near them. Now think it over and see what you can do, because disaster is hanging over our master and his whole household. He is such a wicked man that no one can talk to him."

Abigail lost no time. She took two hundred loaves of bread, two skins of wine, five dressed sheep, five seahs of roasted grain, a hundred cakes of raisins and two hundred cakes of pressed figs, and loaded them on donkeys. Then she told her servants, "Go on ahead; I'll follow you." But she did not tell her husband Nabal.

As she came riding her donkey into a mountain ravine, there were David and his men descending toward her, and she met them. David had just said,

"It's been useless—all my watching over this fellow's property in the desert so that nothing of his was missing. He has paid me back evil for good. May God deal with David, be it ever so severely, if by morning I leave alive one male of all who belong to him!"

When Abigail saw David, she quickly got off her donkey and bowed down before David with her face to the ground. She fell at his feet and said: "My lord, let the blame be on me alone. Please let your servant speak to you; hear what your servant has to say. May my lord pay no attention to that wicked man Nabal. He is just like his name—his name is Fool, and folly goes with him. But as for me, your servant, I did not see the men my master sent.

"Now since the LORD has kept you, my master, from bloodshed and from avenging yourself with your own hands, as surely as the LORD lives and as you live, may your enemies and all who intend to harm my master be like Nabal. And let this gift, which your servant has brought to my master, be given to the men who follow you. Please forgive your servant's offense, for the LORD will certainly make a lasting dynasty for my master, because he fights the LORD's battles. Let no wrongdoing be found in you as long as you live. Even though someone is pursuing you to take your life, the life of my master will be bound securely in the bundle of the living by the LORD your God. But the lives of your enemies he will hurl away as from the pocket of a sling. When the LORD has done for my master every good thing he promised concerning him and has appointed him leader over Israel, my master will not have on his conscience the staggering burden of needless bloodshed or of having avenged himself. And when

the LORD has brought my master success, remember your servant."

David said to Abigail, "Praise be to the LORD, the God of Israel, who has sent you today to meet me. May you be blessed for your good judgment and for keeping me from bloodshed this day and from avenging myself with my own hands. Otherwise, as surely as the LORD, the God of Israel, lives, who has kept me from harming you, if you had not come quickly to meet me, not one male belonging to Nabal would have been left alive by daybreak."

Then David accepted from her hand what she had brought him and said, "Go home in peace. I have heard your words and granted your request."

When Abigail went to Nabal, he was in the house holding a banquet like that of a king. He was in high spirits and very drunk. So she told him nothing until daybreak. Then in the morning, when Nabal was sober, his wife told him all these things, and his heart failed him and he became like a stone. About ten days later, the LORD struck Nabal and he died." (New International Version)

When I read that particular story about Abigail, I'd come to the conclusion, that sometimes it may be necessary for a wife to take certain matters into her own hands to save her household.

Prophetess Lynn and Deacon Brian were both eye witnesses to that confrontational episode that had occurred in the board meeting, and they both provided me with immeasurable, emotional support. I couldn't have been blessed with more dedicated, spiritual children than either of them.

CHAPTER SEVEN

O Wretched Woman That I Am

I was slow to obey the gentle nudging of the Holy Spirit when He had called me numerous times. Meanwhile, I was so self-absorbed in my own plans to continue ministering as 'church mother' in that fellowship, that I attempted to stand my ground in a battle that I could not win. God had spoken, and that should have been the end of it. However, because I didn't want to leave that church when I was first called, God used more drastic measures to get my attention. Like a loving parent, God was telling me, His child, to do something over and over again. My mind, like a child's, was occupied elsewhere and not paying attention to Him.

While I was raising my own children, there were times that I had to repeat my instructions to them quite a few times. When those instructions did not illicit a proper response, I used other methods to get my children's attention. Often, I had to raise the pitch of my voice a few decibels before they would respond, as if they hadn't heard me calling them all along. Annoyingly, I'd ask, "What are you doing that's so important that you can't answer me when I call you!" In retrospect, I wonder if God could have been asking that same question of me. I knew that my children had heard me when I first called them; just as God knew that I

had heard Him when He first called me. He also knew what I was so engrossed in that I didn't acknowledge Him when He was constantly trying to get my attention.

By not following the leading of the Holy Spirit right away, I was disobedient and vulnerable to the attacks of Satan. Soon after that incident, I realized that God was using that particular episode, with all of its ramifications, to chastise and redirect me. I'm reminded of many times when I had to discipline and redirect my children. I still loved them, but whenever they had deliberately disobeyed me, I had to chastise them because of it. I corrected my children because I loved them. I taught them to respect authority, while they were young. I explained to my children that it was for their own good. Long after the chastisement had passed, I wondered if they truly understood that my correcting them was for the purpose of trying to mold an upright character within them so that they would be able to handle responsibility faithfully. Being chastised by God, means that He loves us. His corrections are always for our good.

> *Hebrews 12:6, 11 "The Lord disciplines everyone he loves. He severely disciplines everyone he accepts as his child.... We don't enjoy being disciplined. It always seems to cause more pain than joy. But later on, those who learn from that discipline have peace that comes from doing what is right." (God's Word Translation)*

For thirty-seven years and still counting, my relationship with Jesus has been most satisfying. I've been enjoying sweet fellowship with the Lord. There's nothing about me that's unknown or hidden from Him, including the character flaws that I have. The devil's attacks on my character had the same effect on me as when Job's friends maligned his character. Job ardently defended his relationship with God, even as I vehemently sought to defend my relationship with God when I was called a 'liar'. Apparently, my 'new pastor' thought that I was not even going to make heaven my home. He must surely have known that, according to the Bible, all 'liars' are going to burn in a fiery hell for all eternity. My pride was offended by my pastor's hurtful words. For sometime afterwards, my prayers to the Lord were mingled with tears of self-pity. Looking back, even if I had desired to tell him my feelings, I doubt that he would've wanted to hear them. I knew that while I was dealing with that traumatic experience at the church, that my children were hurting for my sake. However now that they are able to read about my experience and see how the Lord led me through it, they'll understand that it was all for my good. God knows the ending from the beginning and He knows the 'pit-stops' in-between.

My tear ducts must have already dried up when the Holy Spirit was able to bring back to my remembrance some well-known Scriptures relating to a prideful spirit. I had not been quick to follow the Lord's leading, but in pride trying to direct my own way, those Scriptures lifted up a standard of holiness and convicted me of my disobedience. Job didn't know about the existence of Satan as the source of his troubles, but I understood who the culprit behind all of mine was. The devil had used the pastor's false accusations against me. But instead of me allowing God to be my defense, the devil maneuvered me into lashing out in pride with my tongue, to my own defense. The Holy Bible reveals that from before the beginning of time, 'pride' had caused the fall of Lucifer, who is also called Satan and Devil.

> *Isaiah 14: 12-14 How art thou fallen from heaven, O Lucifer, son of the morning! how art thou cut down to the ground, which didst weaken the nations! For thou hast said in thine heart, I will ascend into heaven, I will exalt my throne above the stars of God: I will sit also upon the mount of the congregation, in the sides of the north: I will ascend above the heights of the clouds; I will be like the most High.*

Pride lifted its insidious head during the last board meeting that I attended. Contrary to God's wooing and His efforts to redirect me to spend more time in my nursing home ministry, I was grasping to hold onto my position as 'church mother', refusing to move ahead with God's leading. 'Pride' cunningly slipped in and entrapped me.

Oh, that I had humbled myself with the mind of Christ and had been quick to follow God's leading, those woes could have been avoided.

> *Philippians 2: 5-7 "Have this mind in you, which was also in Christ Jesus: who, existing in the form of God, counted not the being on an equality with God a thing to be grasped, but emptied himself, taking the form of a servant, being made in the likeness of men; . . ."* (American Standard Version)

I believed that my service was still needed as 'church mother' in that ministry, and I thought that my foster daughter, Puggles, who was also a member of the same church fellowship, needed me there. I had been her 'stand-in-mother' for the last seven years, rearing her in the same godly discipline that I'd exercised with my own children. That included seeing that she was in a church where she was being spiritually fed. I was certain that she required pastoral direction for her spiritual growth, and I would have objected strongly to submitting her to the influence of anyone who didn't encourage holy living. When I went to the 'new pastor' to inform him of the immoral conduct that she had gotten herself into, his response was nothing like what I expected to hear from an ordained man of God. I was told that neither I nor anyone else had the right to question Puggles or any other member of the church, concerning their relationship with the Lord. In spite of her immoral conduct, he was ready and willing to allow her to continue participating in the church's dance ministry without cleaning up her life.

> *1 Timothy 6:3-5 "If any man teach otherwise, and consent not to wholesome words, even the words of our Lord Jesus Christ, and to the doctrine which is according to godliness; He is proud, knowing nothing, but doting about questions and strifes of words, whereof cometh envy, strife, railings, evil surmisings, Perverse disputings of men of corrupt minds, and destitute of the truth, . . ."*

I became a Christian while my children were yet very young. I was so blessed and privileged to be able to invest godly principles into their young lives. I realized the importance of teaching my children the principles found in the Holy Bible. By me practicing what I read in the Scriptures, my children were able to see Christ-like behaviors in my life. I told them that people judge others by the conduct that they see in the person's day-to-day living. When we profess that we are Christians, we are encouraged, by the Word of God, to live our lives uprightly before people and before the all-seeing eyes of God.

After teaching my children God's Word, they accepted Jesus, at an early age, as their own personal Lord and Savior. Later as teenagers, they began to pick up sinful habits from their peers; as though they'd forgotten all that they'd been taught. Nevertheless, I continued to pray for them. When they knew that they weren't living right, their consciences didn't allow them to take Holy Communion. They realized that their lives were out of sync with what they'd read and been taught from God's Word. I was grateful to know that they were taking God's Word seriously, and I took that opportunity to inquire of them as to why they had not taken communion.

My foster daughter had also been taught from God's Word, so when her lifestyle ran contrary to the godly lifestyle required by the Scriptures, she also refused to partake of Holy Communion. I questioned her as to what she'd done, and she shared with me why she had not participated in the communion of the Lord's Supper.

I prayed with her just as I'd prayed with my own children when they were growing up. My service as 'church mother' often led me to encourage church members in spiritual matters with their families, and also to give 'motherly-advice' in the same manner as I'd given to my children and to my foster daughter.

I first realized that my ministry of love was going to include being a 'repairer of the breach' when Puggles, an eleven years old girl, was placed in my home by the Division of Youth and Family Services (DYFS). She had been separated, as a toddler, from her biological mother and family. Then being transferred from home to home fourteen different times, she was emotionally bruised and battered when she arrived at my home. I noticed right away that Puggles was suffering emotionally and even though she was quiet and withdrawn, her attitude was malicious and quite noticeable. She didn't hide her feelings on what she thought about her case workers or any of the social workers and therapists who visited with her. Often she had to be reprimanded by me for blurting out nasty remarks about a person to their face or behind their back. Puggles didn't care about her appearance and had to be reminded often about her personal hygiene. I wasn't worried about the responsibility of caring for her in the beginning, because she was only supposed to be in my home for a short period of time. However, I became very concerned when I realized that a few months had already passed and she was still in my care.

The Division of Youth and Family Services (DYFS) asked me if I would be able to extend my care of this child in my home until the end of that school year in June. Since the child was going to be with me a lot longer than I had first thought, I decided that if I disciplined her to improve her behavior and personal hygiene, we might be able to get along together in my home. It wasn't very long after that that I realized how much I didn't like that unruly child. Her attitude let me know that she didn't like me either. After a few more months, I regretted that I had agreed to keep her for an extended time, until that school year ended.

The Holy Spirit encouraged me to love that child, and to look beyond her faults even as God had looked beyond mine. So instead of sending her back into the system, I decided to work patiently with her as God had worked patiently with me through the years. I doubted that there would be a family who would willingly accept a teen whose behavior was so unruly, as hers was. She would definitely need to be placed in a group-home for girls, if I did not continue caring for her. I made up my mind that I would learn to love that unlovable child, if it killed me. I didn't die physically, but dealing with that child, I sometimes felt like I was losing my mind. I often questioned myself, "Why did I leave myself open for such a struggle? I don't need this!" If it wasn't for the love of God, I would've given up on her many-a-time. One by one my valuables began to disappear. They had never turned up missing before Puggles came to live with me. Even her case worker's cell phone mysteriously disappeared when he came to see her on one of his routine monthly visits. Without a doubt I knew that Puggles had taken my possessions, and a few months later the case worker's cell phone was discovered amongst Puggles belongings. When questioned, she swore that she had not taken my money or any of the other items that were deemed to be missing; just like she had sworn that she had not taken the case worker's cell phone. Secretly I was hoping that she would confess and return my stuff to me, but she stuck to her lies and didn't own up to doing anything wrong. I prayed even more for her than I'd been praying, giving all of my disappointments to the Lord. Maybe He trusted her, but I surely didn't.

I'll never forget about the countless late nights that I got into my car, depending on Jesus to lead and direct me as I drove around our town, looking for Puggles. I remember the time when Puggles asked me if she could go to an un-chaperoned house party. I told her that she couldn't go, but she disobeyed me and snuck out of the house and went to that party anyway. If God had not directed me to where she was so late that night, oh, what trouble she might have gotten herself into. When Puggles went to school, she seemingly got into fights everyday, and she would curse out her teachers at the slightest provocation. Her school counselors telephoned to tell me about her fist fights, and about her cursing at her teachers, and that she'd been so disruptive in class. I was at my wits' end to know what I could do to help her change her terrible conduct and attitude, so I prayed for guidance.

The school term quickly passed and I encountered more problems with Puggles when she was able to get a part-time job in a local fast food establishment. One afternoon, Puggles left home, telling me that she was going to her part-time job. When she was late returning home, I began calling and leaving messages on her cell phone. I'd called her numerous times, but when she didn't answer her cell, I became concerned and went to Puggles' job. The manager told me that she had not worked on that afternoon and wasn't even on the schedule to work until the weekend. I was almost hysterical with worry wondering where she could possibly be. When her manager saw how distressed and upset I was, he told me about a group of kids that lived in the area that she had begun hanging out with during her break. He directed me to a building right across the street where a group of kids were sitting on the steps. I went and began questioning the kids about Puggles, and immediately I felt in my spirit that she was hiding in the group amongst her friends, laughing at me. Very annoyed, I said to them that if they see Puggles, just tell her that her grandmother was looking for her and she needs to call home. Immediately I called DYFS to let them know that she had left home, and her case worker instructed me to call the police right away. I had notified these authorities because, as far as I knew, she was missing, and I hoped that she had not met with any foul play. Not wanting to cause alarm to anyone else, I waited a couple of days before I called our pastor to let him know that Puggles was missing from home.

Our pastor located her a few days later and coaxed her into letting him return her back home. He told her that the police were searching for her and that if she allowed him to return her home, she was not going to be in any trouble. After that episode was over and she was safely home again, she confided in me, "Grandma, me and my friends saw you when you first came across the street. They got around me to hide me, and we were laughing at you," she said with a snicker, "because you looked so funny." They all had known me as Puggles' grandmother, so they knew to gather around her when they saw me coming.

I remembered that I used to pray with my children before they left for school, so I began praying with Puggles everyday before she left for school. I never imagined that those prayers would cause such positive changes to happen so quickly. The wonderful transformation that took place in her life has given me an opportunity to share the fruitful outcome of prayer with you, my readers. Each day before Puggles left for school, I would take her hands into mine and we would ask God, together, to keep her from fighting with anyone, to keep her tongue from using profanity, and to keep her hands from stealing anything that didn't belong to her. I felt the anointing of the Lord's presence as we prayed. I'd always end our prayers by letting her know that her angels 'Goodness' and 'Mercy' were on each side of her to help her behave. I told Puggles that her angels would let me know how well she behaved in school that day, and that she would be rewarded if she didn't get a bad school report on that day from any of her teachers. The Holy Spirit led me to give her gifts that she would own; such as, having her own cell phone. I let her know, ahead of time, that her disobedience or bad conduct would cause me to restrict her privilege to use that phone. I never realized how by giving her something to own, that the pride of ownership would influence her behavior for the better. Not only did the child's life change, but, mine did also.

Puggles' behavior changed drastically by respecting her teachers and other adults, by being less disruptive in her classes, and she even stopped fighting with her peers. She went with me to the church that I attended, however, after we began praying together, she actually became involved in the youth activities at the church. I was surprised when she told me how much she liked going with me as I ministered at the nursing homes. My life changed as I grew closer to the Lord and experienced the wonder-working power of prayer. The Bible says that the prayers of a righteous person are effective. I've always prayed throughout the years for my children, grandchildren, and family members and I've experienced the joys of answered prayers for Puggles.

> *James 5: 16 "…make it your habit to confess your sins to one another and to pray for one another, so that you may be healed. The prayer of a righteous person is powerful and effective."* (International Standard Version)

A relationship of love, trust and mutual respect gradually developed between us. After Puggles accepted Jesus as her personal Savior, we both relied on the Holy Spirit to direct our lives. With time, she was able to bond well with my immediate and extended families; inheriting uncles, aunts and a whole host of cousins who love her dearly.

Having dealt with Puggles in the past, with all of her problems, I'm better able to reach out to my grandchildren and other children in their generation who are now facing peer pressure problems. I'm glad that I didn't give up on Puggles, when our relationship was so rocky. I didn't think that I could ever make a difference in her life. On my own I wouldn't have been able to make a difference, but, God could and He did. I have become much more alert to Satan's tactics, lest pride slip in to weaken and destroy my relationships with others and hinder my relationship with God.

We are warned by the Scriptures to avoid the hidden traps that Satan might use to ensnare us. If we are not watchful, we can be so easily overtaken by a prideful spirit. *(Galatians 6:3)* A call of service from God is a call to serve the needs of others. All of our help comes from the Lord. In church, if we are elevated to a position of service in which we are able to help others, we must do so with humility. I have been called by God to fulfill His purposes for my life, but, if I should begin to think more highly of myself than I ought to, I would be opening the door of my mind for the devil and his spirit of pride to enter.

Oh wretched woman was I when in a moment of inattentiveness, I let my guard down, becoming so self-absorbed in my desire to continue holding onto my position as 'church mother'. I believed that when the 'new pastor' took his position as shepherd over the church, he may have felt insecure of his leadership ability. Since the administrative board had been serving for quite awhile in leadership capacity, he may even have felt intimidated and challenged by their years of experience within the ministry.

As 'church mother', I had been highly respected and esteemed by my former pastor and members. My opinions were always valued. I was highly offended by the fact that the 'new pastor' didn't have the slightest clue as to what place of service a 'church mother' filled. How could he appreciate my service, if he knew nothing about the ministry in which God had called me to serve? In a flash of prideful arrogance, I decided to stay to demonstrate to him the duties of a 'church mother'. When I had gone to tell him about the behavior of my foster daughter, Puggles, I had already observed his children and had come to the conclusion that his own household was not in order. In my household, my children abided by my rules, which included attending church faithfully.

Over the years, I've observed a few pastors who did not hold back from preaching about the unruly or immoral conduct of some of the parishioner's children. Yet, those same pastors had a

'blind-spot' when it came to believing the reports of ill-conduct that involved their own children. Often they became highly defensive and made excuses for the trouble that their child(ren) had become involved in. Like a defense attorney, the pastor would charge that the fault lay with the other child who, supposedly, had imposed a bad influence on his child. Another weak defense tactic was to throw up a smoke-screen that suggested that the witness was somewhat mistaken in the facts that they had presented. If the complaining witness persisted, that person was labeled a "busybody" or a "fault-finder". It is a very popular misconception that ostriches hide their heads in the sand when danger approaches. In the case involving my foster daughter, instead of the pastor conducting a thorough investigation to provide the necessary discipline to correct the situation, he symbolically 'shoved his head in the sand' and the problem was ignored. Oh, the terrible judgment that befell the two sons of the ancient High Priest Eli, because of Eli's unwillingness to enforce godly standards within his own household. *(1 Samuel 2: 22-36)*

In my recollection of some of my former pastors, the late Dr. Donald Womack stands out as the man of God who instilled a firm biblical foundation in me during the time when my children were young and most impressionable. I was a member of his church for more than fifteen years. He was unlike the ancient High Priest Eli who was responsible for raising his two sons to serve God in ministry, but had failed to do so. Dr. Womack took responsibility and not only raised his sons, but taught me how to raise my son and three daughters to serve God by his excellent parenting example.

At one time, I had concerns about the behavior of one of his sons, so I addressed him with my concerns. His son was in leadership, representing many youths. He was a young man, still in his teens; nevertheless he was under his father's authority, as were my children under mine. I did not want my children to look at the behavior of the pastor's son and think that, if he could get away with what he was doing without any consequences, then my children could also behave in ways that were not appropriate for Christians and not have to suffer any consequences. I told the late Dr. Womack that it bothered me that his son was ministering to the people in music, while his son's behavior was not becoming of a Christian. He told me that he was not aware of what had taken place in the matter that I was referring to, but that he would investigate the matter. I knew that he dealt with that situation quickly, because his son was soon relieved of his ministerial duties until after he got his affairs straightened out. However, the High Priest Eli on the other hand, didn't deal with the behaviors of his sons because he regarded his sons higher then he regarded the Lord. God declares that those who honor Him, He would honor and those who despise Him, would be lightly esteemed. *(1 Sam 2: 29, 30)* It was the teachings of the late Dr. Donald Womack that led me to know that according to the Bible, God holds parents responsible for training and reprimanding their children, whether or not their children may be holding a position in the ministry.

Reflecting on the incident that dealt with one of the late Dr. Womack's sons, caused me to realize how much he must have loved his children, because Proverbs 3: 12 says "…whom the Lord loveth he correcteth; even as a father the son in whom he delighteth." I was blessed to have been under the ministry of that man of God who not only preached the gospel but also used the Scriptures in disciplining his own children. His preaching also helped me to know how to use the Scriptures as my guideline in disciplining my children.

CHAPTER EIGHT

Hold My Bible

Early on in my walk with Jesus, I learned that the Lord, who is strong and mighty, would fight all of my battles. However, on one particular occasion, my fearless 'sister-in-Zion', who happened to be my natural sister, was about to fight for me. I had never seen anything, or had an experience like that before or since that time.

My sister and I had been saved for a short time and everything about Christianity was exciting to us. We were eager to learn all that we could about our new life, and about our brothers and sisters in the Lord. We began going to tent meetings, seminars, conferences, revivals, and to many other places that we heard that the saints of God would be worshipping the Lord. In many of these services we witnessed deliverances from alcoholism, drug addictions, deafness, blindness and all sorts of diseases. We saw demon—possessed people healed so often by the minister laying his or her hands on the person and praying for them, that we began exercising our faith by laying hands on those who were oppressed by demons too. By acting in line with God's Word, even the demons were subject to us. Many were healed and delivered when we prayed for them. So when we were informed that a good, old-fashioned revival was going to be in town, and the evangelist was Rev. W. V. Grant, we could hardly wait to attend. My sister and I, and our nine children piled into the station wagon and went downtown into the heart of Newark, to the Symphony Hall. The service was all that we'd expected. After we'd seen God use Rev. W.V. Grant to preach the gospel, bring forth a word of prophesy, pray for the sick, we saw the lame walk and witnessed miracles of deaf ears being opened. When the service concluded we were ready to leave from our seats, high up in the balcony. Because so many people were in the service, seated on the ground level, the balcony seats were the only seats available for all of us to be seated together. The service ended and we were walking into the aisle, when a woman who had been seated a few rows behind us, began saying something to our children. When I questioned them as to what the woman had said to them, they responded, "That lady's crazy. She was talking to herself the whole time during the service". When she saw me talking to the children, she came closer to where I was standing. Walking behind me, she began pushing and hitting me in my back and making agitated sounds. I realized that woman was indeed behaving like she had a mental problem. I assumed that she was deranged, so I directed the children to walk quickly in front of me, putting myself between the children and her. We were almost the last people remaining in the balcony area, as others were already crammed together on the ramp that led to the lower level staircase. Traffic was moving at a snail's pace. Sometimes I was able to move out of her reach, but as she got closer to me she continued pushing and punching me in my back. I pushed the children so that they would walk a little faster. When my sister had almost been knocked over by our children, she looked back to see why we were pushing her to move any faster. At one point the woman came closer and really punched me harder in my back. My sister didn't see what was happening to me. But I called out to her saying, "Something's wrong with this woman. She keeps hitting me! This lady's got demons". When my sister heard that, she turned and came around behind me, standing between me and the woman. My sister then directed me to continue walking ahead with the children. The woman began hitting my sister, at which time my sister turned to face the woman and tried reasoning with her. There was no way to get through to that woman, as she continued her irrational behavior. Every time my sister tried to distance herself, this woman would walk faster to catch up to my

SMILE BANDAGES, REPAIRERS OF THE BREACH

sister to continue her aggressive behavior of punching my sister in her back.

After repeated provocation, my sister stopped and looked directly at that woman, and began pleading the blood of Jesus against that demonic spirit. Then my sister, with a stern look on her face, said to me, "Buggie, hold my Bible". I took my sister's Bible and asked her, "What are you going to do, pray for her?" She looked at me without a smile, and said just as calmly as she possibly could, "No. I'm going to beat the devil out of this woman". I looked at my sister, in shock and disbelief. The children looked at my sister and then we burst out laughing. As the woman scurried in the opposite direction, my sister began laughing too. The next thing I remember, my sister, me and all of our children were in the lobby talking and laughing about how my sister was about to 'beat the devil out of that lady'. We laughed like we were crazy. I don't quite remember what happened after that. That was the funniest thing that I remember ever happening to me at an old-fashioned revival. On the other hand, that disruptive confrontation, with my pastor during the last board meeting, that I attended, was the worst thing that ever happened to me as a church member. Nevertheless, I felt unburdened and free when my resignation from the church had become effective. Then a rekindling of the Holy Spirit's fire filled me with an anointing to answer the calling that God had already placed on my life. That anointing came with such power and strength that I felt renewed with the energy that I had had as a young woman.

Throughout the years that I'd been mothering my own children, mothering children of others and serving as 'church mother', God all along had even greater plans for my future. I never would've thought that doing something that comes so naturally, like mothering my own children, could have such positive effects in the lives of others. I had no idea that I could make a difference in the life of any child other than the impact that I had made in the lives of my own children. Having become a foster parent and having invested into the lives of children, and making a difference in their lives, such as in Puggle's case, it has become apparent to me that God has been enlarging my mothering territory to extend into the delicate ministry of serving as a "repairer of the breach". God had begun using me in restoring wholeness and giving a sense of belonging to those needing to be nourished and cherished within a loving family environment.

It has been rewarding as well as challenging for me to stand in the gap for mothers by raising their children, whose lives were full of uncertainty. From the moment of their births, some of the children have been snatched from the unsteady arms of their mothers to be placed into a system that was just as unstable as their mother's arms had been.

Those who would stand in the gap, as 'stand-in-parents' for children who had been separated from their own biological parents, were dedicated people prepared by God to be 'repairers of the breach'. Puggles, is a young adult now, who you may remember, had been separated from her family as a toddler. She was also a ward of the state, and by the time she was placed with me, she had lived in all kinds of environments. Children really need stability and security in their lives to enable them to thrive in a society that has turned many away from the things of God.

I knew of the trauma of a physical breech birth, but I'd never even realized that the separation of a child from his mother and family is considered a 'breach' in the family network. The narrowly avoided breech birth that I went through so many years ago pales in comparison to the physical and emotional breach experienced by many children who are torn from their birth families.

The child, Puggles, who had been placed into my home by (DYFS) had been traumatized by having been taken from her family and then shifted from one temporary family to another, fourteen times, before she came to her last stop in my home. In medical scenarios, doctors are often sought to supervise and render good prenatal care, which is often responsible for preventing or reversing a threatening breech birth. In unavoidable situations, doctors may be called upon to perform a Caesarean section in advance or to repair the damages caused by a breech birth. In both instances, and especially in breech-birth cases, God is the giver of the knowledge and wisdom to successfully handle the delicate problems surrounding those births.

In human relationships, God calls and empowers 'foster parents', as myself and others, to be 'repairers of the breach'; to heal and restore broken or impaired lives with the Holy Spirit's help. Many times, decisions are made early in the life of a child in hopes that they will be placed into a stable, loving, and secure home. In Puggles case, had she not been previously placed with so many different families, she might not have been placed with me as a last resort. DYFS has set aside my home and a few other dedicated homes, to take care of medically fragile children and children with chronic dysfunctional behaviors.

By the time Puggles' was brought to me, I had already begun using blessed oil to anoint the foster children who had become a part of my family. My prayer partners and I would meet at 6:00 am by phone, to pray diligently for my four foster children and others who had been placed into the foster care system. God miraculously answered our prayers for two of our foster children. They had the good fortune of being placed with their prospective, adoptive parents around the same time that Puggles was being placed with me. I didn't realize that with God's guidance, my home would be the home that raised Puggles to adulthood.

As two adult women, Puggles and I often talked together. One day, while Puggles and I were talking, she told me that she hardly ever goes to church anymore. Even though I was disappointed that she was no longer faithfully attending church, I wasn't at all surprised. Puggles' boyfriend was not a Christian. I had spoken to her many times, saying that she really shouldn't be dating someone who wasn't even attending church. I knew that peer pressure could be very persuasive; so much so, that many youths have done things and have gotten into relationships that they can not handle. I was aware that Puggles may have been dealing with some immoral issues when I saw that she had refused to take Holy Communion one Sunday when she had attended church. When Puggles was still living with me, there wasn't much of anything that I didn't know about her, since she would confide in me, telling me about herself as well as about her friends. I shared the gospel of Jesus Christ with her unsaved friends and her boyfriend as well, praying that they all would receive Jesus as their Lord and Savior.

Before leaving the church, I had a conversation with the 'new pastor', concerning Puggles' participation in the praise dance ministry. I strongly believed that anyone whose lifestyle ran contrary to the Word of God should not be allowed to participate in the praise dance ministry. It seemed to me that this time, as at other times when the 'new pastor' had already made his decision, that he had selective hearing.

In my home, over the front door, for many years there hung a plaque with the Scripture verse of *Joshua 24:15*, "…as for me and my house, we will serve the LORD". When my children reached adulthood, and felt that they didn't want to follow my house rules any longer, they had my permission to find a place of their own. Puggles was over eighteen when she moved out of my home. I knew by her new living arrangement, that she was not practicing righteous living accordingly to God's Word. The 'new pastor', evidently, didn't have godly principles written over the 'door posts' of his church, so he didn't have a problem allowing Puggles to dance along with the praise dance ministry while continuing in her immoral lifestyle. He may have thought that by permitting her to continue participating in the dance ministry that she would remain with the church. By me bringing Puggles up as I had reared my own children, I knew that if she didn't have a mind to live according to the Bible, regardless of what she was allowed to do in church, she wasn't going to stay there.

When the 'new pastor' had actually listened to me during one of our later conversations, I told him that even though I would be leaving the church, I would still support the ministry because my husband was still a member of that church fellowship. He questioned whether I really believed that my husband would stay at the church after I had left. I had no intentions of telling my husband or anyone else why I felt the sudden need to leave the church. Some of the church members, who questioned as to why I was no longer attending services at church, were only told that the Lord had called me to another assignment, outside of the church. I did not want anyone to think that I had ill-feelings against the 'new pastor' and I assured him that even though I was leaving the church, my husband would continue coming to the church.

God alone knows what I really felt like during that whole ordeal, and how embarrassing it was for me. I didn't want to tell anyone in the church, exactly, how disrespectful the 'new pastor' and I were towards one another. Even though, I had retaliated and called him a 'liar' after he'd called me one, still, I felt just terrible about the whole thing. Looking back at everything that has happened to me, I know that had I not gone through those experiences, I'd not be as actively involved in the nursing home ministry as I am now. I knew all along that one day I would be evangelizing in a ministry beyond the confines of a church building. I just never imagined that it would be a ministry that would involve children after all of my children were adults. Whenever I felt as if I were drowning in certain situations, and I didn't know what decisions I should make, the Holy Spirit would comfort me by bringing to my mind the passage of Scripture in

Romans 8: 28 that says ... *"we know that all things work together for good to them that love God, to them who are the called according to his purpose."* I knew that that passage in the Bible wasn't there only for me, but it speaks to all of God's children. If all that I went through worked out for good according to God's plan for me, then, it would also work out according to God's plan for the 'new pastor' as he continued repairing breaches through ministering the gospel. Even though I was no longer a member of his church, my husband continued to attend there. I learned from my husband and others of the continuing growth in the ministry and of the positive changes that have been taking place in the church after I left. I heard that he has been preaching messages of holiness with the anointing and power. When my husband and I attended the church's anniversary banquet, the pastor and I engaged in mutually encouraging and uplifting conversation. At that time, he asked me if I would come back to the church, because he said that I was really missed. I told him that I believed that it was all in God's plan and timing for me to have left when I did. I realized that in addition to my foster parenting, God was also expanding my nursing home ministry that involved the children doing liturgical dancing. As occasions would arise there would be opportunities for me to fellowship, along with my husband, with that same body of believers. So, I assured the pastor that I would try to fellowship with his ministry from time to time.

At one point, while I was raising my children, it suddenly dawned on me that I was doing the work of an evangelist. While training and ministering the gospel to them, even though they were my first priority, I could hardly wait until they were grown so that I could work elsewhere in the field of evangelism. My experiences with my children and other children have developed my character to a gourmet texture and richness of dedication and purpose, comparable to the rich flavor and smooth texture of the finest of wines and cheeses that have gone through the aging process.

My years of experience have sharpened my skills in dealing with children and God has opened a way for me to continue serving Him through my ministry to children. I never thought that I would have a desire to be working with children at this stage in my life, however, by being the grandmother of my children's children and to many other children, and realizing that there is a need for them to be ministered to, I've accepted the challenge. I'm willing to invest into the lives of my grandchildren and other children in their generation and to other upcoming generations.

In this age of computers and other gadgets that compete for a young person's time and attention, as a Christian grandmother, I'm challenging the children to embrace the values of God, family life, and fun. I realize that it's a sacrifice for me, because I'm at the age where most women have a desire to relax and take it easy, having already raised all of their children. When I think about all the negativity that surrounds my grandchildren in this wicked and rebellious generation, I'm horrified. For this cause I'm encouraged to seek God's guidance to enable me to reach out to their generation through ministering to them as a "repairer of the breach".

While raising Puggles, I had envisioned that one day she would be working alongside me in my ministry. During the time that Puggles was with me she had become a Christian, and having an up-beat personality, she was very effective in ministering as she worked with the youths in the church. However when she became an adult and moved out on her own, it was heartbreaking to me when I saw that she no longer attended church faithfully. The 'repairers of the breach' reach out to children who have lost their way, usually through no fault of their own.

In hopes of closing the generation gap that exists, I'm recruiting children to join along with the 'Smile Bandages' ministry to demonstrate love to senior citizens, especially those who reside in the neighboring nursing homes and senior facilities. Visiting seniors who readily welcomed God's love wasn't difficult. However, taking youths with me who didn't have an understanding about God or His love was quite challenging. Had I not had the experience of demonstrating love while seeing the changes that took place in Puggle's life, I would not have had the patience or confidence to continue demonstrating love to those children as they struggled to develop Christ-like characters. My grandchildren, nieces, nephews, cousins, and other children in the dance ministry knew and loved Puggles, so I'm constantly reaching out to her and encouraging her to come back to the Lord so that He can use her again to work with the youths. Just when I began to think that all of my meddling and prayers had been to no avail, in a soft voice, Puggles pleaded with me one day, "Don't give up on me, Grandma". "I will never give up on you. I will always love you" was my tender reply to her.

One day soon, I hope that Puggles will come back to assist me with the children who are in my dance troupes. She is younger than I and closer in age to the children. Naturally, they would enjoy having her work with them during their vigorous dance practice sessions.

Psalm 71: 17, 18 "O God, thou hast taught me from my youth: and hitherto have I declared thy wondrous works. Now also when I am old and greyheaded, O God, forsake me not; until I have shewed thy strength unto this generation, and thy power to every one that is to come".

Puggles had often shared with me her desires of one day ministering to the up-coming generations of youth. I'm constantly reminding Puggles of those dreams that she had shared with me. I make myself available to her, and by keeping in touch with her, I'm hopeful that she will return to the faith and fulfill her heart's desires.

CHAPTER NINE

Grandma's Vision: A Camp Ministry

After my children began having their own children, I was proud to be a grandmother. However, I was unable to be the traditional grandmother to my grandchildren, because I was quite busy pampering and being a 'stand-in-mother' to the children in my foster care. The children that I cared for were medically fragile and mentally challenged and their needs required much of my time. The other children that I fostered, who were not handicapped, began calling me grandma. Because the majority of my time needed to be given to the children who were living in my household, I discouraged my children from asking me to babysit for them. As my grandchildren got older they didn't require as much pampering from me, so I was able to keep them at my home for a couple of weeks during the summer. Having all of my grandchildren at my home became a bonding time for them to know one another and a time for me to bond with each of them. As time passed, some of my children and their families moved away from New Jersey, the state in which I live. Nevertheless, once my grandchildren were out of school for the summer, every effort was made by their parents for me to continue having 'grandma's time' with the grandchildren.

In July 2009 I busily prepared for the arrival of the grandchildren at my home to spend part of their summer vacation with me. I know that they would have a great time at 'Grandma's Camp', which is what they had begun calling their yearly family reunion times at my house. They would love sleeping under the stars in the heavy-duty tent that they would help me set up. They would swing back and forth, and round and round, on the old tire that hangs from one of the large tree branches in my backyard. The grandkids would jump up and down and do flips on the trampoline. They would search for twigs and tiny sticks in the yard and gather them into neat little piles to be used later to build open campfires and have wiener roasts and marshmallow roasts. They would make s'mores by putting roasted marshmallows and pieces of Hershey's chocolate bars, sandwiched between two graham crackers. Playing volley ball and having ping pong matches and whatever other games they could make up, kept them active outdoors. A bonus activity for the grandkids would be swimming in my backyard pool throughout the day to cool off from the heat of the hot summer sun, and then later into the early evening as an added treat before retiring for the night. I know they would engage in these activities, because they enjoyed them at 'Grandma's Camp' last year.

My grandchildren usually come around late July and the beginning of August, but with two of my daughters expecting birth additions into their families, my grands came to visit with me three weeks early. Because I purposed to take a major role in the lives of my grandchildren and other children, I began taking them along with me to nursing homes and other senior-facilities where I minister. Some amazing things began happening. Not only did I witness the joyful expressions on the faces of the seniors and the children as they sang songs along with the seniors and danced for them, but I was thrilled when one of my grandsons expressed to me that making the seniors happy makes him happy too.

In summers gone by, I'd taken my grandchildren with me when I had visited the seniors in the nursing homes, but I'd expected this summer would be more rewarding because God had given me some brand, new ideas for my ministry. The previous summer my grandchildren danced with the Smile Bandages 'Jewels' praise dancers; a dance troupe that I'd started for the sole purpose of taking children with me to encourage and entertain the seniors. With the rapid growth of youths desiring to join up with the nursing home praise dancers, God inspired me to divide the group and start a separate, step dance troupe for the boys. I was thrilled with this new extension, as God was enlarging my territory. All of my grandsons participated in the launching of this new ministry extension which is called 'Smile Bandages Salvation Stompers' dance troupe. This name was given to the group by one of my grandsons. Having a desire to infuse godly character into the lives of my grandchildren and other children has prompted me to take them to nursing homes to share the love of God with the seniors who are unable to come out to a church building for worship services. On the first and fourth Sundays of each month, the children who are in my dance troupes interact with the seniors by dancing for them and talking and smiling with them. This interaction brings joy to both the seniors and the children. Hearing the laughter and seeing the smiling faces assures me that the generation gap is fast being replaced by love and understanding.

God makes it very clear in His Word that we ought to love our neighbors as we love ourselves. However, loving my neighbors, according to what the Bible says, has proven to be somewhat of a challenge for me. I've always been shy and usually I would withdraw from people because it wasn't easy for me to show love to people I didn't know. On the other hand, it's the most natural thing in the world for me to express love to my children, grandchildren, family members and even to my friends. As I came to know my in-laws and distant relatives, I began loving them. It was essential that we spend quality time together to build a strong relationship that would enable us to bond with one another in love, and show the affection that we say we have for each other. It's a privilege for me to communicate with my family members and friends, whom I love dearly. I've later come to understand that only by having a loving relationship with God can I really express to anyone else how genuine my love for them really is.

> *John 15:12 "This is my commandment, That ye love one another, as I have loved you."*

As my relationship with the Lord developed, I began to understand the values that God desired for me to make a part of my life. Therefore, I found it difficult for me to approve of those whose behaviors were different from mine, running contrary to the values that I was trying to instill in my children. I loved my children unconditionally, even though they didn't always have good behaviors. But, it was not easy for me to love other children who posed the threat of influencing my children with their bad behaviors. Now that I'm a grandmother, I'm motivated even more to yield myself to God for His instructions on how I should go about trying to instill godly character into the lives of my grandchildren and others in the upcoming generations. I believe that God is still directing my steps, even as He had given me instructions for my children years ago.

With great determination to have the new dance ministry launched before the grandchildren's stay at my camp came to its end, I was overjoyed to have Prophetess Lynn Smith assist me in preparing the boys for their step dancing. We only had a little more than two weeks to work with them before they'd be performing at the nursing home on the fourth Sunday in July. Their ages ranged from four to fourteen, so much patience was needed to keep the boys motivated and encouraged to practice regularly.

Besides running errands for supplies for the camp, which is what I usually do, I had to take over my sister Patricia's duties as camp counselor because she was unable to come this year. One of the main duties, besides many other things, that she usually handled was seeing to it that the children were busy doing fun-activities. I thought that I'd be lost without having the tactful wit that my sister usually provides for my grandchildren, but I declare that Prophetess Lynn was a God-send. Not only did Prophetess Lynn provide fun-filled-activities for my grandchildren to participate in, but, with my oldest granddaughter, Da-Veia, assisting her, Prophetess Lynn prepared the boys to perform like mighty soldiers of valor. By making sure that the children were having fun, Prophetess Lynn freed me from the most important duty of a camp counselor. She made sure that the children practiced their dance steps and had fun too. That released me to run errands for the supplies for the camp, and to find proper uniforms for the dance 'stompers' to wear.

SMILE BANDAGES, REPAIRERS OF THE BREACH

My granddaughter, Da-Veia, is a very talented writer of poetry. She composed a rap, using a few Scriptures from the Bible books of Psalm and Proverbs. The following rap poetry is what she composed and taught to the Smile Bandages 'Salvation Stompers' for them to recite at their first performance at the nursing home at the end of July, in 2009.

The Lord is my light
He protects me through the night
When darkness comes near
I know not to fear
Hold unto the Lord
And keep Him by your side
When evil comes around
You don't have to run and hide

We're persecuted from day to day
'cause of the words we'll never say
They try to turn our love to hate
But we'll hold onto You for You know our fate

Uno, Dos, Tres, Cuatro, Cinco, Seis
Six things that the Lord hates
Prideful eyes
A tongue that lies
Innocents dying at evil hands
Hearts making up wicked plans
Feet quickly rushing into evil's fire
Fakes that lie to get their desires

Your beginning has always been
Your ending will forever be
You're the God over the universe
And the God over me

By Da-Veia Antoinette Brown

This summer was one of the best times ever that I had with my grandchildren. God made it all possible by sending Prophetess Lynn alongside me to help me instill unforgettable godly character principles into them. They will remember the competition games she taught them while building godly character into them as they worked together as teammates. They will not forget the encouragement she gave to them for completing a task that she requested of them, even though they may have lost that particular game. They were encouraged to cheer their teammates on during the 'spoon and egg' races so that they would move more swiftly. They learned that races are not always won by the fastest runners, as in the 'water-races', but by the ones who listen and follow directions and have more water in their cups at the end of the race. All of the children learned to be tolerant and patient with one another.

The task of ministering the gospel to today's youth is not an easy venture, and I'm not deceiving myself into believing that it is. It wasn't an easy task when I shared the gospel with my children, and I'm sure it will be quite an experience for me now with my grandchildren. Times are much worse now than they were when I was growing up, and have worsened since the time when I was bringing up my children. Now, people have become lovers of themselves more than they are lovers of God. With each generation, people get increasingly more wicked and devious as they draw farther away from God. When my children were very young, I sheltered them as much as I could from the evil behaviors that I saw the non-believers engaging in, and I was diligent to teach my children biblical principles.

Shortly after we moved into a new neighborhood, an incident happened that seemed to rip my heart right out of me. Although, I never discouraged my children from going out to play with other children, when my children played amongst themselves, I didn't have to constantly be at my window or at my door to watch out for them. My son, the eldest of my four children, was outside with his sisters one day playing a chasing game. The front of our yard was unfenced, so they were running around the house, through the gate to the back of the house and around the opposite side of the house into the front yard. I'd just checked on them and saw that they were having a good time. After a few minutes, when I next checked on them again, I was shocked to see a much larger boy, whose height towered over all of the other children that were with him, bullying my little children. I heard him threatening my babies that if they ran around the house one more time, he was going to hit them.

My children were friendly and they had already begun making a few friends with some of the neighbors' children. However, the devil had targeted them, on that particular day, to be harassed by this kid who didn't even live in the neighborhood. My heart ached to the core, when I saw my little ones trembling in fear, not knowing how to fight or defend themselves. I had never taught my children to hit, kick, or spit at other children who may have done those things to them. Since becoming a Christian, I had always tried to keep my kids under my close supervision. My husband and I would have heated arguments, when he would insist that our children retaliate. Yet, I was busy teaching my children the Golden Rule, and training them to be kind to others. My children were naïve. I kept a close watch on them when they played with other children, so as to keep their sense of innocence from becoming tainted. They didn't realize that their acts of kindness might sometimes be repaid by cruel or unkind acts.

Instead of chasing each other in fun, my children slowly cowered backwards to sit on the front steps of our house. Meanwhile, a group of neighborhood boys had gathered on the sidewalk in front of my house. Unable to watch any longer, I walked over to the boy, shaking my pointer finger at his nose, screaming, "The blood of Jesus against you! I rebuke you in the name of Jesus!" When I began praying aloud in my prayer language, that child froze in his tracks. Then everybody ran away as fast as they could, leaving me to comfort my children. I took them inside the house with me for a few hours and only let them back outside when I was able to be with them. A day or two later, that very same boy came alone looking for me. "Lady," he questioned with a frightened look on his face, "What was that curse that you put on me?" I laughed within myself before answering him. "I didn't put a curse on you, honey" I said softly. "I cursed the spirit of the devil that was using you to bully my children." I continued talking to the boy about the devil and about God, for about ten or fifteen minutes more. I don't remember seeing him very much after that incident, except when he visited with his cousins who lived across the street from us. That day I didn't only win the battle of protecting my little ones from that bully, but it kept any potential bullies in my neighborhood from rising up against my children. From time to time I invited the neighborhood boys to my home to play Scrabble with me and my children. Although we enjoyed the word game, Scrabble, I had an ulterior motive. By inviting the youths to my home, I was banking on the fact that if I was friendly with those boys, they wouldn't be so quick to pick on my little boy.

Mothers and grandmothers are following a biblical example when they shelter their young children from evil. In biblical times, an angel was sent from the Lord to warn Joseph to take his family to Egypt in order to keep King Herod from finding and killing the young child, Jesus, the only begotten Son of God.

> Matt 2:13 "…the angel of the Lord appeareth to Joseph in a dream, saying, Arise, and take the young child and his mother, and flee into Egypt, and be thou there until I bring thee word: for Herod will seek the young child to destroy him.

The Word of God shelters and strengthens us to stand firm in troublesome situations. The Bible tells us of Timothy's faithful grandmother, Lois, and his faithful mother, Eunice, who instructed him in the faith of God's Word. That godly foundation, laid by his grandmother and his mother, prepared him to take a stand as one of the pastors in the early Christian churches.

I tried to give my children a godly foundation when they were young, and to teach them manners. One day recently, I overheard an adult say "Excuse me", without addressing that apology to any one in particular. At and early age, my children were taught that God watches over them and that He hears and sees everything they do. My mind rushed back many years to recall one of many incidents when I had overheard one of my children breaking wind, just outside my presence, and then reverently apologizing with an "Excuse me, Lord". That reverent awareness of God's presence also occurred on several other occasions when that same child would innocently belch after eating and then she'd remark "Excuse me, Lord" with her very next breath as she cast her eyes upward towards heaven. The power of God uses love and a sound mind to empower a person to act in child-like faith against enemy forces. Surely, God's Word is a shelter for the meek ones who trust in Him to protect and equip them to stand firmly against the devil who would use fear and dread to hinder them.

I'm persuaded that I am answering God's call to set a foundation of faith for the upcoming youth by taking my young dance troupers with me to the nursing homes where I preach the Gospel of Jesus Christ. The children and I give smiles of encouragement to the seniors, and they smile back at us as a testimony that love can be preached with just a smile. As we cheer up the seniors, everyone is touched by God's love including visiting family members and friends who may be in attendance at the service.

I've dedicated myself completely to the seniors and to the children in my dance troupes. The Lord continues to give me new ideas on how to stimulate the seniors whenever we visit with them. As soon as we walk into the dinning hall where the seniors have assembled, they begin their facial and lung-expansion exercises before the children begin to dance for them. The senior's facial exercises consist of them turning in the direction of another person and opening their mouth to tell that other person, "I Love You". They must do that exercise with someone, at least three times. Then they do the lung exercise in which everyone gets really excited as they take a deep breath and sing individually at the microphone "Doe-Re-Mi-Fa-Sol-La-Ti-Doe." After each one has had the opportunity to sing solo, the children then pass out song books and we all begin to sing together. I love it. They love it. We all love it. Even their visiting family members and friends join in and they love it too. The staff feel welcomed to join in and sing with us. During the hour while all of this is going on, the seniors are encouraged to signal for any 'Jewel' or any 'Stomper' or for myself, to give them a hug or just hold their hand. They don't have to ask for a smile, because we always have one for them.

Smile Bandages "Stompers" is a ministry for young boys; their counterpart, the Smile Bandages "Jewels", is a ministry for girls. Both of these dance ministries are comprised of young children; ages fifteen and younger who are under my leadership and guidance. The children are taught the 'Golden Rule', which is to treat others as they themselves want to be treated. The Bible also instructs them to put on the 'whole armor of God' in order to be able to detect and avoid the subtle traps of the devil. They also learn, from the Bible, the importance of first submitting themselves to God and then resisting the temptations of the devil by choosing to do what's right, and refraining from doing what's wrong.

Along with their unique style of dance steps, they recite Scripture verses from the Bible books of Psalm and Proverbs. This combination of dancing and reciting Scripture is a powerful weapon to defeat Satan. As the mission of this ministry is to instill into young children that God really loves them, they are reminded that they are "...fearfully and wonderfully made..." in God's image. *(Psalm 139:14)* They are inspired to spread Jesus' love as they interact with the seniors in the communities around them.

The Smile Bandages "Stompers" and the Smile Bandages "Jewels" bring smiles to the seniors' faces each time they visit with them at the nursing homes. The "Stompers" realize that the "stomping" dance steps, and memorized Scriptures, are reminders to them that they can defeat the devil by their dependence on God and their own actions. The bold dance steps suggest, to the children, that they are able to "stomp on the devil's head" (SOTDH) to his defeat. The Smile Bandages "Jewels" and "Stompers" both provide delightful, ministry entertainment for the seniors at the nursing homes and other facilities where seniors reside. These children also accompany me to other outreaches where I minister. Every first and fourth Sundays, along with the children, I minister at nursing homes in Plainfield New Jersey.

If you have a loved one, residing in a nursing facility in Plainfield or in its immediately surrounding areas in New Jersey, and would like for them to be visited by me and my dance troupes, you may contact me by e-mail at *vertiereid@vertiereid.com* or *vertiereid@verizon.net* I can also be reached by phone at (908) 753-2373

My desire is to live a pleasing life before our Lord and Savior, Jesus Christ. Procrastination and disobedience would love to hinder and block me from going forth to accomplish what God has called me to do. Please continue praying for me. I need your prayers. Not only would I suffer the consequences of not fulfilling my ministry, but others would be deprived of the love that God would have me to share and I know God would not be pleased. As the pages of this book draw to a close, I'd like to ask of you the same thing that I ask of the seniors at the nursing facilities that I visit. Reverently, let's join together in prayer:

Thank You, Lord, for making us fearfully and wonderfully in Your divine image. You have called us to worship and give praises to You. You've shown Your great love for us through the death, burial, and resurrection of Jesus Christ, Your only begotten Son. Your Word teaches us to do to others as we would want others to do to us, and to love our neighbors as we love ourselves. Ungrudgingly, we desire to give You, our God, the highest form of worship that we all can give, as we unselfishly and joyfully offer ourselves in service to the people of Your love. Help us, Lord, to do these things for Your glory.

In the mighty, awe-inspiring name of Jesus, we pray, Amen.

CHAPTER TEN

Photo Gallery

Book signing at Women's Conference 2008
'Smile Bandages cover a Multitude of Pain'

2009 Conference: 'Smile Bandages, Loving the Unlovable' Patricia, our camp counselor, is holding my two published books: 'Smile Bandages Cover a Multitude of Pain' and 'Smile Bandages, Loving the Unlovable'.

"I Love You . . ." Mary calls out

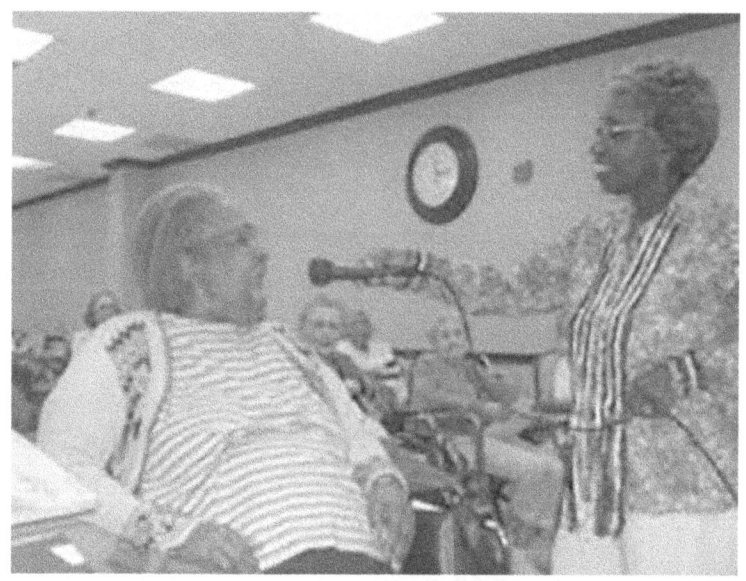

I'm holding the microphone for Cecile while she sings "Doe-Re-Mi-Fa-Sol-La-Ti-Doe"

Noah (left) and CJ (right) are embraced by a resident admirer as three Smile Bandages 'Jewels' stand behind them for this photo

SMILE BANDAGES, REPAIRERS OF THE BREACH

Three of the 'Jewels' circulating among the residents

A Birthday photo taken at the nursing home of 90 year old, Dorothy, sitting next to me

Noah finds the page in the songbook for a nursing home resident

One of the Smile Bandages 'Jewels' give a resident a hug

Grandma Bess' surrounded by her three granddaughters and three praise dancers at a Nursing Home in N.C

Sarah is on the left side of this photo and Ruby's on the right

Me and a Nursing Home resident pose for a photo

A picture taken with a resident at the Genesis Nursing Home, 2009

A photo at the Genesis Nursing Home, 2009

Ms Beverly smiles beautifully, as the residents looks on,
while she poses for a snapshot with the
'Jewels' and the 'Stompers'

**Genesis Nursing Home 'Love Birds' 2009
Rena embraces a resident in a hug**

**Lonnie is on the left side of this photo
and Sarah is on the right**

Nursing Home, 2009
Mattie, 86, her husband, Deacon Samuel Smith,
87 and Me

One resident waits patiently as CJ
turns the page in the songbook

Minnie is surrounded by Smile Bandages 'Jewels' and 'Stompers'

Smile Bandages 'Jewels' and 'Stompers' spending time with seniors

A 'Jewel' is posing with Willa Mae at the Nursing Home, 2009

Smiling for the camera

Looking on with approval while the children dance

Miles said that his name is "Die". Because his son couldn't say 'Dad' when he was young, he called him 'Die'

Three nursing home residents wait for the children to dance

Sally, a nursing home resident, poses with me for a photo

Rena's posing for a photo with resident at the nursing home

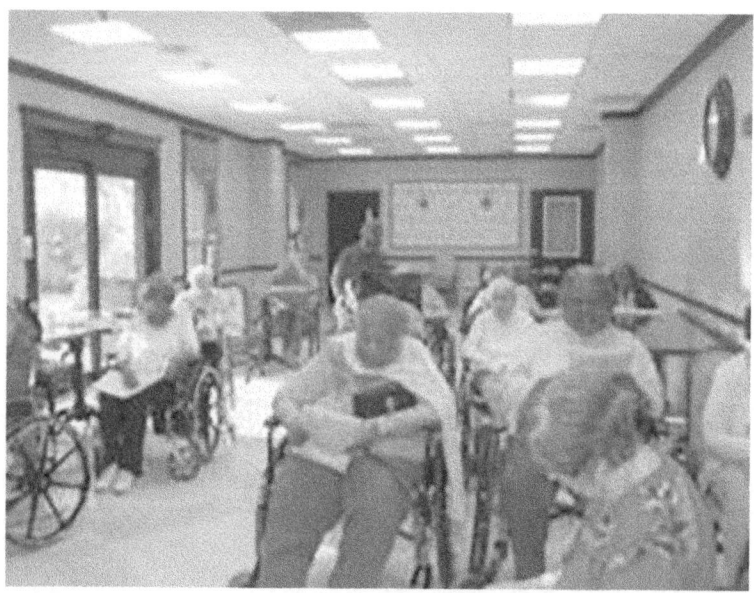

Residents gather for a singing session at the nursing home

SMILE BANDAGES, REPAIRERS OF THE BREACH

Looking for the right page in the songbook

Watching the Smile Bandages 'troupes' dance

(from left to right)
My foster daughter, Puggles, T.V. anchor woman, Della Cruz, And me, and my grandson, Clarence Jr.

A book signing at Barnes and Nobles
That's my book that Dr Creflo Dollar is holding.

Da-Veia Antoinette Brown, our poet

Prayer Circle

The Water-Race

Is That Egg Glued to The Spoon?

SMILE BANDAGES, REPAIRERS OF THE BREACH

Silent Socks

'When we realized that our 'silent socks' couldn't make any 'stomping sounds,' we had to throw on our shoes. Smile Bandages 'Stompers' July 2009

Ready! Camera!...Action!
Smile Bandages 'Stompers' July 2009

**Minister Helynne Smith poses with the Smile Bandages 'Stompers'
July 2009**

**A Mother's Smile of Pride
Smile Bandages 'Stompers' July 2009**

Two 'Jewels', pose for a photo with me Brittany
on the left and Tiffany on the right

'Future Jewel'
The 'Jewels' and 'Stompers' gather 'round as my daughter,

Dashawn, poses with her 16 month old daughter, Harmony, my youngest grandchild. Summer of 2009

Smiles from my husband, Randy, and my son, Allen July 2009

**Cooling off in the swimming pool
at Grandma's Camp is fun**

Two cousin, Da-Veia (left) and Jasmine (right), put their heads together to strike a pose

Keep digging!
When I saw one of my grandsons digging up my
grass, looking for treasures, I turned that area
into a sandbox, so they could continue digging
for their treasures. Camp time, July 2009

Would you believe that this is the first time that my grandsons cooked on an outdoor grill? They cooked dinner for everyone at camp this summer. Boy was the chicken and burgers delicious! July 2009.

SMILE BANDAGES, REPAIRERS OF THE BREACH

**Cindy and Dashawn embrace, while
Cindy's boyfriend tends to the grill**

**My son, Allen (Charlie),
holding his little cousin, Jaden, on his lap**

**Volley Ball Teams: Girls against the boys
Where's the ball? ... Where're the boys?**

**Team Formation
"Little guys to the front ... spread out boys"**

Fun For All
"Look who's on the girls' side...
My daughter, Nicky, and her unborn son, Jordan"

Let's play the game... and talk about it later

Boys and girls competing against one another, let's see which team wins

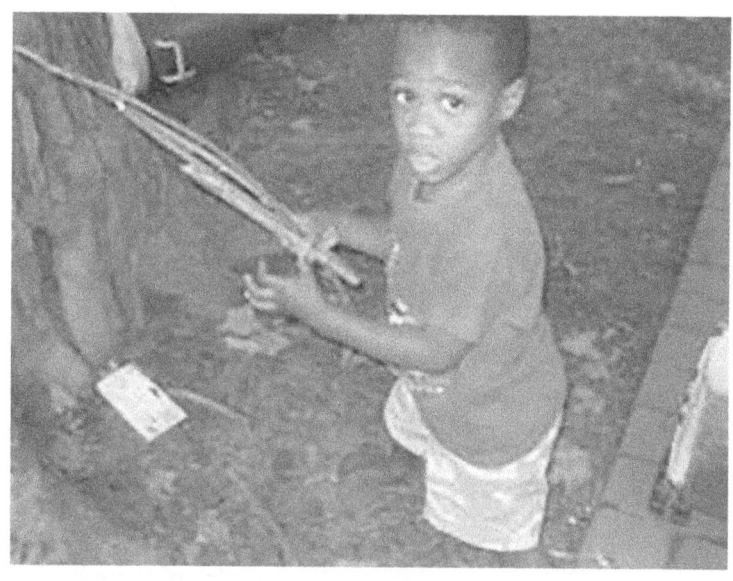

"I got my sticks," says Deon, "for my marshmallow roast"

Anyone for S'mores

A quick photo shot of me and my granddaughter, Anari, July 2009

Asaph Womack, recording music artist who's the son of the late Dr. Donald Womack.

Book Signing
I've got Martha Munizzi's CD, and she's got my book!

Authors' Festival with Marie Lamba

Mayor Cory A. Booker, City of Newark N. J.

Mayor Butrico, City of South Plainfield N.J.

Dr. Alveda King, niece of the late Dr. Martin Luther King, Jr.

Attorney Patrick Bradshaw, So. Plainfield N.J.

Councilmen of South Plainfield Tim McConville (left) and Raymond Setronko, holding my books

Smile Bandages 'Stompers' and 'Jewels' . . . on the move for Christ!

Excerpt from "Smile Bandages, Coping with Irreversible Damages"

All of a sudden, I felt as if the wind had been knocked out of me. I could not believe what this woman was saying to me. A lump formed in my throat and it was very difficult for me to swallow. I blinked hard trying to keep back the tears that were welling up in my eyes. The anger and frustrations I was experiencing, drowned out the concern and interest that the caseworker had spoken of concerning Shandi's welfare. For years, I experienced one problem after another with the Division of Youth and Family Services. Children in foster care can't speak for themselves, so, their caregivers have to speak on their behalf.

Shandi's seven years old, almost eight now, and I've cared for her practically all of her life. When she was about four years old, Shandi's health worsened. DYFS was financially responsible to cover the expenses that Medicare didn't cover. Medicare supplied my home with hospital equipment, and also paid for nurses to provide care twelve hours a day, seven days a week. As her foster parent, I spent many night hours caring for her, since she did not have nurses working throughout the night.

Shandi's health was so fragile that she needed close monitoring. I was like a new mother caring for her delicate, newborn baby. But in reality, I was a sixty-plus year old grandmother who had already raised all of my kids. Shandi was connected to several monitoring machines. Sometimes I would be awakened in the middle of the night by the alarm that would be sounding to alert me that there was either a cardiac or a respiratory problem that I needed to respond to immediately. On some occasions, when I would reach her room, which is right across from mine, one of the machines would be indicating that her heart rate had exceeded its safety limit. I would see her elbows bent and her fingers clenched into tight fists. Her little legs would be drawn up with her toes curled under. It seemed to me that she was experiencing another anxiety attack, with her extremities shaking violently. I would cuddle her in my arms and gently stroke her back, while I rocked slowly back and forth with her while whispering into her ears, "Shandi, calm down baby. I love you. It's gonna be alright". Gradually, her heart rate would return back to normal, and the alarm would silence itself. On other occasions, the respiratory monitor might be alarming to indicate that she was not breathing properly, or that the tubing had somehow become disconnected from the CPAP respiratory mask that rested on her face to cover her nose. 'CPAP' is a humidified, forced air ventilation system used by some patients diagnosed with sleep apnea. On some rare occasions, she was just experiencing a period of sleep apnea, which is one of her medical diagnoses. It was only by the mercies of God that I was able to properly care for Shandi.

Before Shandi's health had begun deteriorating, I seldom asked the Division of Youth and Family Services to provide an alternate home for respite care for Shandi. When I needed to take a vacation, I chose to take Shandi along with me everywhere. However, when it became too much of a health risk for Shandi to be with me when I had to travel a long ways from home, I had to leave her behind with nurses to monitor and care for her until I returned.

Sitting on my living room sofa, across from me, was a young woman who was now Shandi's new caseworker. Although she had been in my home a few times before, we had not yet bonded in a relationship of trust. Shandi's former caseworker had been seeing Shandi in my home for the last five years and she was the one who had brought to my attention that DYFS was now pushing for me to adopt Shandi. They were placing emphasis on getting handicapped children out of the foster care system and into family adoptions, if possible. This new caseworker was harping on that same issue, and I really didn't want to hear it. She was presenting me with the harshest ultimatum I could've imagined: adopt Shandi or be ready to surrender her to be placed in an institution. I had hoped that day would never come, certainly I was not prepared, nor expecting it at this time. After all, I'd been caring for her since she was eight months old.

I'd just completed my third book. I didn't criticize about the faltering foster care system in that book, as I'd done in my first two books. As a matter of fact, I was thinking about whether I should become an advocate for foster care for the sake of the many children who are in that government system. I didn't think that the Division of Youth and Family Services could do or would say anything to me that would hinder me from doing the work that I was certain that God had called me to do. Now I was wondering. "My God, what am I supposed to do now?"

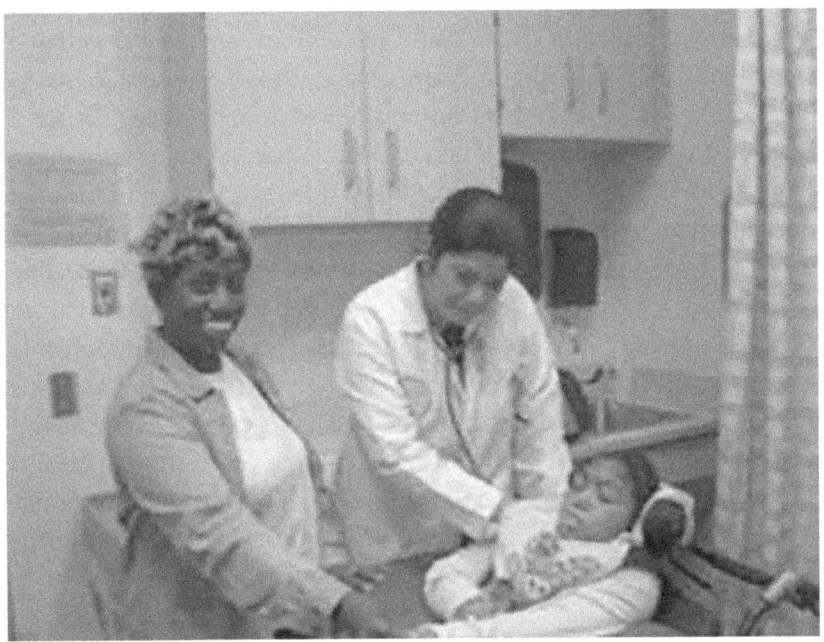

Maya Ramagopal, MD, Shandi's, respiratory doctor

My life stopped being my own when I realized that I never owned it in the first place. Once I understood that I was fearfully and wonderfully made in the image of God, I tried to live my life according to how God's Word says I should live as a follower of Christ. I was created to give Him praise and to fellowship with Him. I believed what God's Word said about me and I began doing what the Lord said that I should do with my life. It took a long time for me to realize God's purpose and calling in my life. However, when I finally recognized it, I began going full force into the ministry. I believe that it was in His plan from the very beginning of my conception.

God blessed me with four adorable children within the space of six years. I realized they were the spitting image of me and my husband. It was a few years into their young lives when they began growing up that God got my full attention. His Word assured me that my children were fearfully and wonderfully made in His image just as I was. I looked at each of those magnificent beings and came to the only conclusion that I could've come to, and that was that I needed guidance in caring for them. Motherhood was new to me.

As a child, I had helped my mother with my siblings. When I gave birth to my children I was not given a manual on how to make them whole in their spirit, soul, and body. I was a young, unmarried mother when I gave birth to two healthy children. I was married by the time I gave birth to the next two of my healthy children. The man, whom I married, didn't know as much as I did about caring for those precious gifts from the Lord that we were now responsible to nurture and take care of. He had not helped his mother with his siblings as I had helped my mother with my siblings. My husband was the youngest of his mother's three children. Even though he and I both were raised in a home without either of us having our father in our lives, our views of the responsibilities of a father, towards his children, were as different as night and day. However, for us, it worked out in our favor. I learned quickly how to depend on the Lord's guidance in parenting my children without over-stepping the boundaries of my husband's authority. God was preparing me for a ministry that would cater to His most valuable gifts; children. And I learned to love it.

Not long after learning that Jesus would be a friend that I could tell anything, I made a confession about myself that I've shared with only a few others who I felt that I could trust with my most private secrets. I was sure that if my innermost secrets were revealed, more than likely, it would hinder me from having a normal relationship with anyone.

I carried many of those secrets into my marriage. I was certain that if they were revealed, my marriage would not stand the shock. By being truthful in all of my confessions to Jesus, I have a healthy relationship not only with my husband, but I also enjoy sweet fellowship with the Lord. While rearing our four children, I was confronted with a couple of those secrets that I had confessed to the Lord. Had I not yielded to the Holy Spirit to correct them, those damaging secrets could have hindered my ability to nurture my children or anybody else's children.

Now I must seek God's peace concerning the decision of the Division of Youth and Family Services to disrupt Shandi's living with me in my home. A hurried decision could do irreversible damage to Shandi, possibly leading to a situation that might bring about wrongful death due to negligence, if she's not placed in an environment where she'll receive the extensive care and attention that she needs.

Also available from this author, "Smile Bandages Cover a Multitude of Pain and Smile Bandages, Loving the Unlovable"

www.ingramcontent.com/pod-product-compliance
Ingram Content Group UK Ltd.
Pitfield, Milton Keynes, MK11 3LW, UK
UKHW022226230426
12048UKWH00016BA/1090